M Macaulay

LAYS OF ANCIENT ROME.

BY

THOMAS BABINGTON MACAULAY.

EDITED, WITH NOTES,

BY

WILLIAM J. ROLFE, LITT. D.,

AND

JOHN C. ROLFE, PH. D.

WITH ENGRAVINGS.

NEW YORK ·:· CINCINNATI ·:· CHICAGO

AMERICAN BOOK COMPANY

ENGLISH CLASSICS.

EDITED BY WM. J. ROLFE, LITT. D.

Illustrated. 12mo, Cloth, 56 cents per volume.

SHAKESPEARE'S WORKS.

The Merchant of Venice.	Richard III.
Othello.	Henry VIII.
Julius Cæsar.	King Lear.
A Midsummer-Night's Dream.	The Taming of the Shrew.
Macbeth.	All 's Well that Ends Well.
Hamlet.	Coriolanus.
Much Ado about Nothing.	The Comedy of Errors.
Romeo and Juliet.	Cymbeline.
As You Like It.	Antony and Cleopatra.
The Tempest.	Measure for Measure.
Twelfth Night.	Merry Wives of Windsor.
The Winter's Tale.	Love's Labour 's Lost.
King John.	Two Gentlemen of Verona.
Richard II.	Timon of Athens.
Henry IV. Part I.	Troilus and Cressida.
Henry IV. Part II.	Pericles, Prince of Tyre.
Henry V.	The Two Noble Kinsmen.
Henry VI. Part I.	Venus and Adonis, Lucrece, etc.
Henry VI. Part II.	Sonnets.
Henry VI. Part III.	Titus Andronicus.

GOLDSMITH'S SELECT POEMS.   BROWNING'S SELECT POEMS.
GRAY'S SELECT POEMS.   BROWNING'S SELECT DRAMAS.
MINOR POEMS OF JOHN MILTON.   MACAULAY'S LAYS OF ANCIENT ROME.
WORDSWORTH'S SELECT POEMS.

LAMBS' TALES FROM SHAKESPEARE'S COMEDIES.
LAMBS' TALES FROM SHAKESPEARE'S TRAGEDIES.

EDITED BY WM. J. ROLFE, LITT. D.

Illustrated. Cloth, 12mo, 50 cents per volume.

Lays of Ancient Rome.

W. P. 8

PREFACE.

AT the request of the publishers, the first name on the title-page of
this book is that of the editor of the "English Classics" series in which
it is included ; but the better part of the work has been done by his son,
John C. Rolfe, Professor of Latin in the University of Pennsylvania.
The senior editor has arranged the introduction, compared the text
with the English editions and revised its punctuation, and helped in
seeing the book through the press. The Notes are almost entirely the
junior editor's, having received only occasional revision in minor points
at the hands of his senior.

The editors are fully agreed in the opinion that parallel reading in
English should accompany the study of Latin in our high schools and
academies, where, especially in the preparatory course for college, so
little time can be given to purely literary training. For such reading
Macaulay's *Lays* are particularly well-adapted, both on account of their
subjects and their many allusions to Roman customs and habits, and
also, to our thinking, for their poetical merit. Certain critics, of whom
the late Matthew Arnold is perhaps the most noteworthy, tell us that
the *Lays* are not poetry ; but in this instance we are content to be wrong
with John Stuart Mill and Henry Morley and "Christopher North" (see
pages 140, 143 below) and Edmund Clarence Stedman, if they *are* wrong,
rather than to be right with Matthew Arnold, if he *is* right. Every teacher
who has used the *Lays* with his classes can testify that boys enjoy them
heartily. They have long been a part of the *curriculum* in the Boston
Latin School and other of our best preparatory schools, and are included
in the English reading required for admission to Harvard and other colleges. No doubt they would have been more generally introduced into
schools but for the lack of an annotated edition. As Macaulay says
(page 29 below), the learned reader does not need notes on the *Lays*, and
for the unlearned they would have little interest ; but the schoolboy needs
them, and the average teacher is not "learned" enough to dispense with
them in all cases. In preparing the present volume the editors have

repeatedly been compelled to hunt up for themselves allusions on which classical instructors and professors were unable to give them help.

The Notes being mainly intended for the schoolboy, the quotations from classical authors have been drawn as far as possible from those read in preparatory schools. Explanations are also given of many points in ancient geography, history, institutions, manners, etc., which, even if the young folk have already learned them or could look them up in other books, it may be well to make readily accessible—if only as a review— in connection with the text of the poems. The occasional notes on Eng-lish etymology are intended only as hints to teachers who are not already in the habit of letting their pupils dig a little among vernacular "roots" as well as Greek and Latin ones.

W. J. R.

CONTENTS.

ROMAN SOLDIERS.

THE TIBER.

INTRODUCTION

TO

MACAULAY'S LAYS OF ANCIENT ROME.

I. THE AUTHOR'S PREFACE.

THAT what is called the history of the kings and early consuls of Rome is to a great extent fabulous, few scholars have, since the time of Beaufort, ventured to deny. It is certain that, more than three hundred and sixty years after the date ordinarily assigned for the foundation of the city, the public records were, with scarcely an exception, destroyed by the Gauls. It is certain that the oldest annals of the commonwealth were compiled more than a century and a half after this destruction of the records. It is certain, therefore, that the great Latin writers of the Augustan age did not possess those materials without which a trustworthy account of the infancy of the Republic could not possibly be framed.

Those writers own, indeed, that the chronicles to which they had access were filled with battles that were never fought and consuls that were never inaugurated; and we have abundant proof that, in these chronicles, events of the greatest importance—such as the issue of the war with Porsena, and the issue of the war with Brennus—were grossly misrepresented. Under these circumstances, a wise man will look with great suspicion on the legend which has come down to us. He will, perhaps, be inclined to regard the princes who are said to have founded the civil and religious institutions of Rome, the son of Mars and the husband of Egeria, as mere mythological personages, of the same class with Perseus and Ixion. As he draws nearer and nearer to the confines of authentic history, he will become less and less hard of belief. He will admit that the most important parts of the narrative have some foundation in truth. But he will distrust almost all the details, not only because they seldom rest on any solid evidence, but also because he will constantly detect in them, even when they are within the limits of physical possibility, that peculiar character, more easily understood than defined, which distinguishes the creations of the imagination from the realities of the world in which we live.

The early history of Rome is indeed far more poetical than anything else in Latin literature. The loves of the Vestal and the God of War; the cradle laid among the reeds of Tiber; the fig-tree; the she-wolf; the shepherd's cabin; the recognition; the fratricide; the rape of the Sabines; the death of Tarpeia; the fall of Hostus Hostilius; the struggle of Mettus Curtius through the marsh; the women rushing with torn raiment and dishevelled hair between their fathers and their husbands; the nightly meetings of Numa and the Nymph by the well in the sacred grove; the fight of the three Romans and the three Albans; the purchase of the Sibylline books; the crime of Tullia; the simulated madness of Brutus; the ambiguous reply of the Delphian oracle to the Tar-

quins ; the wrongs of Lucretia ; the heroic actions of Horatius
Cocles, of Scævola, and of Clœlia ; the battle of Regillus, won
by the aid of Castor and Pollux ; the defence of Cremera ;
the touching story of Coriolanus ; the still more touching
story of Virginia ; the wild legend about the draining of the
Alban lake ; the combat between Valerius Corvus and the
gigantic Gaul—are among the many instances which will at
once suggest themselves to every reader.

In the narrative of Livy, who was a man of fine imagination, these stories retain much of their genuine character.
Nor could even the tasteless Dionysius distort and mutilate
them into mere prose. The poetry shines, in spite of him,
through the dreary pedantry of his eleven books. It is discernible in the most tedious and in the most superficial modern works on the early times of Rome. It enlivens the dul-
ness of the *Universal History*, and gives a charm to the most
meagre abridgments of Goldsmith.

Even in the age of Plutarch there were discerning men
who rejected the popular account of the foundation of Rome,
because that account appeared to them to have the air, not
of a history, but of a romance or a drama. Plutarch, who
was displeased at their incredulity, had nothing better to say
in reply to their arguments than that chance sometimes turns
poet, and produces trains of events not to be distinguished
from the most elaborate plots which are constructed by art.*
But though the existence of a poetical element in the early
history of the Great City was detected so many ages ago,

---

* Ὕποπτον μὲν ἐνίοις, ἐστὶ τὸ δραματικὸν καὶ πλασματῶδες · οὐ δεῖ δὲ
ἀπιστεῖν, τὴν τύχην ὁρῶντας, οἵων ποιημάτων δημιουργός ἐστι. — *Rom.*
viii. This remarkable passage has been more grossly misinterpreted
than any other in the Greek language, where the sense was so obvious.
The Latin version of Cruserius, the French version of Amyot, the old
English version by several hands, and the later English version by Lang-
horne are all equally destitute of every trace of the meaning of the original.
None of the translators saw even that ποίημα is a poem. They all ren-
der it an event.

the first critic who distinctly saw from what source that poetical element had been derived was James Perizonius, one of the most acute and learned antiquaries of the seventeenth century. His theory, which in his own days attracted little or no notice, was revived in the present generation by Niebuhr, a man who would have been the first writer of his time if his talent for communicating truths had borne any proportion to his talent for investigating them. That theory has been adopted by several eminent scholars of our own country, particularly by the Bishop of St. David's, by Professor Malden, and by the lamented Arnold. It appears to be now generally received by men conversant with classical antiquity ; and, indeed, it rests on such strong proofs, both internal and external, that it will not be easily subverted. A popular exposition of this theory, and of the evidence by which it is supported, may not be without interest even for readers who are unacquainted with the ancient languages.

The Latin literature which has come down to us is of later date than the commencement of the second Punic war, and consists almost exclusively of works fashioned on Greek models. The Latin metres, heroic, elegiac, lyric, and dramatic, are of Greek origin. The best Latin epic poetry is the feeble echo of the *Iliad* and *Odyssey*. The best Latin eclogues are imitations of Theocritus. The plan of the most finished didactic poem in the Latin tongue was taken from Hesiod. The Latin tragedies are bad copies of the masterpieces of Sophocles and Euripides. The Latin comedies are free translations from Demophilus, Menander, and Apollodorus. The Latin philosophy was borrowed, without alteration, from the Portico and the Academy; and the great Latin orators constantly proposed to themselves as patterns the speeches of Demosthenes and Lysias.

But there was an earlier Latin literature—a literature truly Latin—which has wholly perished, which had, indeed, almost wholly perished long before those whom we are in the habit of regarding as the greatest Latin writers were born. That literature abounded with metrical romances, such as are found in every country where there is much curiosity and intelligence, but little reading and writing. All human beings not utterly savage long for some information about past times, and are delighted by narratives which present pictures to the eye of the mind. But it is only in very enlightened communities that books are readily accessible. Metrical composition, therefore, which in a highly civilized nation is a mere luxury, is in nations imperfectly civilized almost a necessary of life, and is valued less on account of the pleasure which it gives to the ear than on account of the help which it gives to the memory. A man who can invent or embellish an interesting story, and put it into a form which others may easily retain in their recollection, will always be highly esteemed by a people eager for amusement and information, but destitute of libraries. Such is the origin of ballad-poetry, a species of composition which scarcely ever fails to spring up and flourish in every society at a certain point in the progress towards refinement. Tacitus informs us that songs were the only memorials of the past which the ancient Germans possessed. We learn from Lucan and from Ammianus Marcellinus that the brave actions of the ancient Gauls were commemorated in the verses of bards. During many ages, and through many revolutions, minstrelsy retained its influence over both the Teutonic and the Celtic race. The vengeance exacted by the spouse of Attila for the murder of Siegfried was celebrated in rhymes, of which Germany is still justly proud. The exploits of Athelstane were commemorated by the Anglo-Saxons, and those of Canute by the Danes, in rude poems, of which a few fragments have come down to us. The chants of the Welsh harpers preserved, through ages of darkness, a faint and doubtful memory of Arthur. In the Highlands of Scotland may still be gleaned some relics of the old songs about Cuthullin and Fingal. The long struggle of the Servians against the Ottoman power was recorded in lays full of martial spirit.   We learn from Herrera that, when a Peruvian Inca died, men of skill were appointed to celebrate him in verses, which all the people learned by heart and sang in public on days of festival.   The feats of Kurroglou, the great freebooter of Turkistan, recounted in ballads composed by himself, are known in every village of Northern Persia. Captain Beechey heard the bards of the Sandwich Islands recite the heroic achievements of Tamehameha, the most illustrious of their kings.   Mungo Park found in the heart of Africa a class of singing-men, the only annalists of their rude tribes, and heard them tell the story of the victory which Damel, the negro prince of the Jaloffs, won over Abdulkader, the Mussulman tyrant of Foota Torra.   This species of poetry attained a high degree of excellence among the Castilians before they began to copy Tuscan patterns.   It attained a still higher degree of excellence among the English and the Lowland Scotch during the fourteenth, fifteenth, and sixteenth centuries.   But it reached its full perfection in ancient Greece ; for there can be no doubt that the great Homeric poems are generically ballads, though widely distinguished from all other ballads, and, indeed, from almost all other human compositions, by transcendent sublimity and beauty.

As it is agreeable to general experience that, at a certain stage in the progress of society, ballad-poetry should flourish, so is it also agreeable to general experience that, at a subsequent stage in the progress of society, ballad-poetry should be undervalued and neglected.   Knowledge advances ; manners change ; great foreign models of composition are studied and imitated.   The phraseology of the old minstrels becomes obsolete.   Their versification, which, having received its laws only from the ear, abounds in irregularities, seems licentious and uncouth.   Their simplicity appears beggarly when compared with the quaint forms and gaudy coloring of such artists as Cowley and Gongora.   The ancient lays, unjustly despised by the learned and polite, linger for a time in the memory of the vulgar, and are at length too often irretrievably lost. We cannot wonder that the ballads of Rome should have altogether disappeared, when we remember how very narrowly, in spite of the invention of printing, those of our own country and those of Spain escaped the same fate. There is, indeed, little doubt that oblivion covers many English songs equal to any that were published by Bishop Percy, and many Spanish songs as good as the best of those which have been so happily translated by Mr. Lockhart. Eighty years ago, England possessed only one tattered copy of *Childe Waters* and *Sir Cauline*, and Spain only one tattered copy of the noble poem of *The Cid.* The snuff of a candle, or a mischievous dog, might, in a moment, have deprived the world forever of any of those fine compositions. Sir Walter Scott, who united to the fire of a great poet the minute curiosity and patient diligence of a great antiquary, was but just in time to save the precious relics of the Minstrelsy of the Border. In Germany, the *Lay of the Nibelungs* had been long utterly forgotten, when, in the eighteenth century, it was for the first time printed from a manuscript in the old library of a noble family. In truth, the only people who, through their whole passage from simplicity to the highest civilization, never for a moment ceased to love and admire their old ballads were the Greeks.

That the early Romans should have had ballad-poetry, and that this poetry should have perished, is therefore not strange. It would, on the contrary, have been strange if these things had not come to pass; and we should be justified in pronouncing them highly probable even if we had no direct evidence on the subject. But we have direct evidence of unquestionable authority.

Ennius, who flourished in the time of the second Punic war, was regarded in the Augustan age as the father of Latin poetry. He was, in truth, the father of the second school of

Latin poetry, the only school of which the works have descended to us. But from Ennius himself we learn that there
were poets who stood to him in the same relation in which
the author of the romance of *Count Alarcos* stood to Garci-
laso, or the author of the *Lytell Geste of Robyn Hode* to
Lord Surrey. Ennius speaks of verses which the Fauns and
the bards were wont to chant in the old time, when none
had yet studied the graces of speech, when none had yet
climbed the peaks sacred to the goddesses of Grecian song.
" Where," Cicero mournfully asks, " are those old verses
now ?" *

Contemporary with Ennius was Quintus Fabius Pictor, the
earliest of the Roman annalists. His account of the infancy
and youth of Romulus and Remus has been preserved by
Dionysius, and contains a very remarkable reference to the
ancient Latin poetry. Fabius says that, in his time, his countrymen were still in the habit of singing ballads about the
Twins. " Even in the hut of Faustulus "—so these old lays
appear to have run—" the children of Rhea and Mars were,
in port and in spirit, not like unto swineherds or cowherds,

---

*   " Quid ?   Nostri versus ubi sunt?
      . . . ' Quos olim Fauni vatesque canebant,
      Cum neque Musarum scopulos quisquam superarat,
      Nec dicti studiosus erat ' " (*Brutus*, xxii.).

The Muses, it should be observed, are Greek divinities. The Italian
goddesses of verse were the Camœnæ. At a later period, the appellations were used indiscriminately ; but in the age of Ennius there was
probably a distinction. In the epitaph of Nævius, who was the representative of the old Italian school of poetry, the Camœnæ, not the Muses,
are represented as grieving for the loss of their votary. The " Musarum
scopuli " are evidently the peaks of Parnassus.

Scaliger, in a note on Varro (*De Lingua Latina*, lib. vi.), suggests, with
great ingenuity, that the Fauns, who were represented by the superstition of later ages as a race of monsters, half gods and half brutes, may
really have been a class of men who exercised in Latium, at a very remote period, the same functions which belonged to the Magians in Persia and to the bards in Gaul.

but such that men might well guess them to be of the blood of kings and gods." *

* Οἱ δὲ ἀνδρωθέντες γίνονται, κατά τε ἀξίωσιν μορφῆς καὶ φρονήματος ὄγκον οὐ συοφορβοῖς καὶ βουκόλοις ἐοικότες, ἀλλ᾿ οἵους ἄν τις ἀξιώσειε τοὺς ἐκ βασιλείου τε φύντας γένους, καὶ ἀπὸ δαιμόνων σπορᾶς γενέσθαι νομιζομένους, ὡς ἐν τοῖς πατρίοις ὕμνοις ὑπὸ Ῥωμαίων ἔτι καὶ νῦν ᾄδεται (Dion. Hal. i. 79). This passage has sometimes been cited as if Dionysius had been speaking in his own person, and had, Greek as he was, been so industrious or so fortunate as to discover some valuable remains of that early Latin poetry which the greatest Latin writers of his age regretted as hopelessly lost. Such a supposition is highly improbable; and, indeed, it seems clear from the context that Dionysius, as Reiske and other editors evidently thought, was merely quoting from Fabius Pictor. The whole passage has the air of an extract from an ancient chronicle, and is introduced by the words Κόϊντος μὲν Φάβιος, ὁ Πίκτωρ λεγόμενος, τῇδε γράφει.

Another argument may be urged which seems to deserve consideration. The author of the passage in question mentions a thatched hut which in his time stood between the summit of Mount Palatine and the Circus. This hut, he says, was built by Romulus, and was constantly kept in repair at the public charge, but never in any respect embellished. Now, in the age of Dionysius there certainly was at Rome a thatched hut, said to have been that of Romulus. But this hut, as we learn from Vitruvius, stood, not near the Circus, but in the Capitol (Vit. ii. 1). If, therefore, we understand Dionysius to speak in his own person, we can reconcile his statement with that of Vitruvius only by supposing that there were at Rome, in the Augustan age, two thatched huts, both believed to have been built by Romulus, and both carefully repaired and held in high honor. The objections to such a supposition seem to be strong. Neither Dionysius nor Vitruvius speaks of more than one such hut. Dio Cassius informs us that twice, during the long administration of Augustus, the hut of Romulus caught fire (xlviii. 43, liv. 29). Had there been two such huts, would he not have told us of which he spoke? An English historian would hardly give an account of a fire at Queen's College without saying whether it was at Queen's College, Oxford, or at Queen's College, Cambridge. Marcus Seneca, Macrobius, and Conon, a Greek writer from whom Photius has made large extracts, mention only one hut of Romulus, that in the Capitol (M. Seneca, *Contr.* i. 6; Macrobius, *Sat.* i. 15; Photius, *Bibl.* 186). Ovid, Livy, Petronius, Valerius Maximus, Lucius Seneca, and St. Jerome mention only one hut of Romulus, without specifying the site (Ovid, *Fasti,* iii. 183; Liv. v. 53; Petronius,

Cato the Censor, who also lived in the days of the second Punic war, mentioned this lost literature in his lost work on the antiquities of his country.   Many ages, he said, before his time, there were ballads in praise of illustrious men ; and these ballads it was the fashion for the guests at banquets to sing in turn while the piper played.   " Would," exclaims Cicero, "that we still had the old ballads of which Cato speaks !" *

Valerius Maximus gives us exactly similar information, without mentioning his authority, and observes that the ancient Roman ballads were probably of more benefit to the

Fragm. ; Val. Max. iv. 4 ; L. Seneca, *Consolatio ad Helviam* ; D. Hieron. *Ad Paulinianum de Didymo*).

The whole difficulty is removed if we suppose that Dionysius was merely quoting Fabius Pictor.   Nothing is more probable than that the cabin which, in the time of Fabius, stood near the Circus, might, long before the age of Augustus, have been transported to the Capitol, as the place fittest, by reason both of its safety and of its sanctity, to contain so precious a relic.

The language of Plutarch confirms this hypothesis. He describes with great precision the spot where Romulus dwelt, on the slope of Mount Palatine, leading to the Circus ; but he says not a word implying that the dwelling was still to be seen there. Indeed, his expressions imply that it was no longer there.   The evidence of Solinus is still more to the point.   He, like Plutarch, describes the spot where Romulus had resided, and says expressly that the hut had been there, but that in his time it was there no longer.   The site, it is certain, was well remembered ; and probably retained its old name, as Charing Cross and the Haymarket have done.   This is probably the explanation of the words " casa Romuli " in Victor's description of the Tenth Region of Rome under Valentinian.

* Cicero refers twice to this important passage in Cato's Antiquities : " Gravissimus auctor in Originibus dixit Cato, morem apud majores hunc epularum fuisse, ut deinceps, qui accubarent, canerent ad tibiam clarorum virorum laudes atque virtutes.   Ex quo perspicuum est, et cantus tum fuisse rescriptos vocum sonis, et carmina " (*Tusc. Quaest.* iv. 2).   Again : " Utinam exstarent illa carmina, quae, multis saeculis ante suam aetatem, in epulis esse cantitata a singulis convivis de clarorum virorum laudibus, in Originibus scriptum reliquit Cato " (*Brutus*, xix.).

young than all the lectures of the Athenian schools, and that
to the influence of the national poetry were to be ascribed the
virtues of such men as Camillus and Fabricius.*

Varro, whose authority on all questions connected with the
antiquities of his country is entitled to the greatest respect,
tells us that at banquets it was once the fashion for boys to
sing, sometimes with and sometimes without instrumental
music, ancient ballads in praise of men of former times.
These young performers, he observes, were of unblemished
character, a circumstance which he probably mentioned because, among the Greeks, and indeed in his time among the
Romans also, the morals of singing-boys were in no high repute.†

The testimony of Horace, though given incidentally, confirms the statements of Cato, Valerius Maximus, and Varro.
The poet predicts that, under the peaceful administration of
Augustus, the Romans will, over their full goblets, sing to the
pipe, after the fashion of their fathers, the deeds of brave
captains and the ancient legends touching the origin of the
city.‡

The proposition, then, that Rome had ballad-poetry is not

---

* " Majores natu in conviviis ad tibias egregia superiorum opera car-
mine comprehensa pangebant, quo ad ea imitanda juventutem alacriorem
redderent. . . . Quas Athenas, quam scholam, quae alienigena studia huic
domesticae disciplinae praetulerim ?   Inde oriebantur Camilli, Scipiones,
Fabricii, Marcelli, Fabii " (Val. Max. ii. 1).

† " In conviviis pueri modesti ut cantarent carmina antiqua, in quibus
laudes erant majorum, et assa voce, et cum tibicine " (Nonius, *Assa
voce pro sola*).

‡   " Nosque et profestis lucibus et sacris
                Inter jocosi munere Liberi,
                    Cum prole matronisque nostris,
                    Rite deos prius apprecati,
                Virtute functos, more patrum, duces,
                Lydis remixto carmine tibiis,
                    Trojamque et Anchisen et almae
                    Progeniem Veneris canemus " (*Carm.* iv. 15).

merely in itself highly probable, but is fully proved by direct evidence of the greatest weight.

This proposition being established, it becomes easy to understand why the early history of the city is unlike almost everything else in Latin literature, native where almost everything else is borrowed, imaginative where almost everything else is prosaic. We can scarcely hesitate to pronounce that the magnificent, pathetic, and truly national legends which present so striking a contrast to all that surrounds them are broken and defaced fragments of that early poetry which, even in the age of Cato the Censor, had become antiquated, and of which Tully had never heard a line.

That this poetry should have been suffered to perish will not appear strange when we consider how complete was the triumph of the Greek genius over the public mind of Italy. It is probable that at an early period Homer and Herodotus furnished some hints to the Latin minstrels;* but it was not till after the war with Pyrrhus that the poetry of Rome began to put off its old Ausonian character. The transformation was soon consummated. The conquered, says Horace, led captive the conquerors. It was precisely at the time at which the Roman people rose to unrivalled political ascendency that they stooped to pass under the intellectual yoke. It was precisely at the time at which the sceptre departed from Greece that the empire of her language and of her arts became universal and despotic. The revolution, indeed, was not effected without a struggle. Nævius seems to have been the last of the ancient line of poets. Ennius was the founder of a new dynasty. Nævius celebrated the first Punic war in Saturnian verse, the old national verse of Italy.† Ennius sang the second Punic war in numbers borrowed from the Iliad. The elder poet, in the epitaph which he wrote for him-

---

* See the Preface to the *Lay of the Battle of Regillus*.

† Cicero speaks highly, in more than one place, of this poem of Nævius; Ennius sneered at it, and stole from it.

self, and which is a fine specimen of the early Roman diction and versification, plaintively boasted that the Latin language

As to the Saturnian measure, see Hermann's *Elementa Doctrinae Metricae*, iii. 9.

The Saturnian line, according to the grammarians, consisted of two parts. The first was a catalectic dimeter iambic; the second was composed of three trochees. But the license taken by the early Latin poets seems to have been almost boundless. The most perfect Saturnian line which has been preserved was the work, not of a professional artist, but of an amateur:

"Dabunt malum Metelli Naevio poetae."

There has been much difference of opinion among learned men respecting the history of this measure. That it is the same with a Greek measure used by Archilochus is indisputable (Bentley, *Phalaris*, xi.). But in spite of the authority of Terentianus Maurus, and of the still higher authority of Bentley, we may venture to doubt whether the coincidence was not fortuitous. We constantly find the same rude and simple numbers in different countries, under circumstances which make it impossible to suspect that there has been imitation on either side. Bishop Heber heard the children of a village in Bengal singing " Radha, Radha," to the tune of " My boy Billy." Neither the Castilian nor the German minstrels of the Middle Ages owed anything to Paros or to ancient Rome. Yet both the poem of the Cid and the poem of the Nibelungs contain many Saturnian verses; as,

"Estas nuevas á mio Cid eran venidas."
"Á mí lo dicen; a tí dan las orejadas."

"Man möhte michel wunder von Sifride sagen."
"Wa ich den Künic vinde daz sol man mir sagen."

Indeed, there cannot be a more perfect Saturnian line than one which is sung in every English nursery:

"The queen was in her parlor eating bread and honey;"

yet the author of this line, we may be assured, borrowed nothing from either Nævius or Archilochus.

On the other hand, it is by no means improbable that, two or three hundred years before the time of Ennius, some Latin minstrel may have visited Sybaris or Crotona, may have heard some verses of Archilochus sung, may have been pleased with the metre, and may have introduced it at Rome. Thus much is certain, that the Saturnian measure, if not a native of Italy, was at least so early and so completely naturalized there that its foreign origin was forgotten.

had died with him.* Thus what to Horace appeared to be the first faint dawn of Roman literature appeared to Nævius to be its hopeless setting. In truth, one literature was setting and another dawning.

Bentley says, indeed, that the Saturnian measure was first brought from Greece into Italy by Nævius. But this is merely *obiter dictum*, to use a phrase common in our courts of law, and would not have been deliberately maintained by that incomparable critic, whose memory is held in reverence by all lovers of learning. The arguments which might be brought against Bentley's assertion—for it is mere assertion, supported by no evidence—are innumerable. A few will suffice.

1. Bentley's assertion is opposed to the testimony of Ennius. Ennius sneered at Nævius for writing on the first Punic war in verses such as the old Italian bards used before Greek literature had been studied. Now the poem of Nævius was in Saturnian verse. Is it possible that Ennius could have used such expressions if the Saturnian verse had been just imported from Greece for the first time?

2. Bentley's assertion is opposed to the testimony of Horace. "When Greece," says Horace, "introduced her arts into our uncivilized country, those rugged Saturnian numbers passed away." Would Horace have said this if the Saturnian numbers had been imported from Greece just before the hexameter?

3. Bentley's assertion is opposed to the testimony of Festus and of Aurelius Victor, both of whom positively say that the most ancient prophecies attributed to the Fauns were in Saturnian verse.

4. Bentley's assertion is opposed to the testimony of Terentianus Maurus, to whom he has himself appealed. Terentianus Maurus does indeed say that the Saturnian measure, though believed by the Romans from a very early period ("credidit vetustas") to be of Italian invention, was really borrowed from the Greeks. But Terentianus Maurus does not say that it was first borrowed by Nævius. Nay, the expressions used by Terentianus Maurus clearly imply the contrary; for how could the Romans have believed, from a very early period, that this measure was the indigenous production of Latium if it was really brought over from Greece in an age of intelligence and liberal curiosity, in the age which gave birth to Ennius, Plautus, Cato the Censor, and other distinguished writers? If Bentley's assertion were correct there could have been no more doubt at Rome about the Greek origin of the Saturnian measure than about the Greek origin of hexameters or Sapphics.

* Aulus Gellius, *Noctes Atticae*, i. 24.

The victory of the foreign taste was decisive ; and, indeed, we can hardly blame the Romans for turning away with contempt from the rude lays which had delighted their fathers, and giving their whole admiration to the immortal productions of Greece. The national romances, neglected by the great and the refined whose education had been finished at Rhodes or Athens, continued, it may be supposed, during some generations to delight the vulgar. While Virgil, in hexameters of exquisite modulation, described the sports of rustics, those rustics were still singing their wild Saturnian ballads.* It is not improbable that, at the time when Cicero lamented the irreparable loss of the poems mentioned by Cato, a search among the nooks of the Apennines as active as the search which Sir Walter Scott made among the descendants of the moss-troopers of Liddesdale might have brought to light many fine remains of ancient minstrelsy. No such search was made. The Latin ballads perished forever. Yet discerning critics have thought that they could still perceive in the early history of Rome numerous fragments of this lost poetry, as the traveller on classic ground sometimes finds, built into the heavy wall of a fort or convent, a pillar rich with acanthus leaves or a frieze where the Amazons and Bacchanals seem to live. The theatres and temples of the Greek and the Roman were degraded into the quarries of the Turk and the Goth. Even so did the ancient Saturnian poetry become the quarry in which a crowd of orators and annalists found the materials for their prose.

It is not difficult to trace the process by which the old songs were transmuted into the form which they now wear. Funeral panegyric and chronicle appear to have been the intermediate links which connected the lost ballads with the histories now extant. From a very early period it was the usage that an oration should be pronounced over the remains

* See Servius, *in Georg*. ii. 385.

of a noble Roman. The orator, as we learn from Polybius, was expected, on such an occasion, to recapitulate all the services which the ancestors of the deceased had, from the earliest time, rendered to the commonwealth. There can be little doubt that the speaker on whom this duty was imposed would make use of all the stories suited to his purpose which were to be found in the popular lays. There can be as little doubt that the family of an eminent man would preserve a copy of the speech which had been pronounced over his corpse. The compilers of the early chronicles would have recourse to these speeches ; and the great historians of a later period would have recourse to the chronicles.

It may be worth while to select a particular story, and to trace its probable progress through these stages. The description of the migration of the Fabian house to Cremera is one of the finest of the many fine passages which lie thick in the earlier books of Livy. The Consul, clad in his military garb, stands in the vestibule of his house, marshalling his clan, three hundred and six fighting-men, all of the same proud patrician blood, all worthy to be attended by the fasces and to command the legions. A sad and anxious retinue of friends accompanies the adventurers through the streets ; but the voice of lamentation is drowned by the shouts of admiring thousands. As the procession passes the Capitol, prayers and vows are poured forth, but in vain. The devoted band, leaving Janus on the right, marches to its doom, through the Gate of Evil Luck. After achieving high deeds of valor against overwhelming numbers, all perish save one child, the stock from which the great Fabian race was destined again to spring, for the safety and glory of the commonwealth. That this fine romance, the details of which are so full of poetical truth, and so utterly destitute of all show of historical truth, came originally from some lay which had often been sung with great applause at banquets is in the highest degree probable. Nor is it difficult to imagine a mode in which the transmission might have taken place. The celebrated Quintus Fabius Maximus, who died about twenty years before the first Punic war, and more than forty years before Ennius was born, is said to have been interred with extraordinary pomp. In the eulogy pronounced over his body, all the great exploits of his ancestors were doubtless recounted and exaggerated. If there were then extant songs which gave a vivid and touching description of an event, the saddest and the most glorious in the long history of the Fabian house, nothing could be more natural than that the panegyrist should borrow from such songs their finest touches, in order to adorn his speech. A few generations later the songs would perhaps be forgotten, or remembered only by shepherds and vine-dressers. But the speech would certainly be preserved in the archives of the Fabian nobles. Fabius Pictor would be well acquainted with a document so interesting to his personal feelings, and would insert large extracts from it in his rude chronicle. That chronicle, as we know, was the oldest to which Livy had access. Livy would, at a glance, distinguish the bold strokes of the forgotten poet from the dull and feeble narrative by which they were surrounded, would retouch them with a delicate and powerful pencil, and would make them immortal.

That this might happen at Rome can scarcely be doubted ; for something very like this has happened in several countries, and, among others, in our own. Perhaps the theory of Perizonius cannot be better illustrated than by showing that what he supposes to have taken place in ancient times has, beyond all doubt, taken place in modern times.

" History," says Hume, with the utmost gravity, " has preserved some instances of Edgar's amours, from which, as from a specimen, we may form a conjecture of the rest." He then tells very agreeably the stories of Elfleda and Elfrida, two stories which have a most suspicious air of romance, and which, indeed, greatly resemble, in their general character, some of the legends of early Rome. He cites, as his authority for these two tales, the chronicle of William of Malmesbury, who lived in the time of King Stephen. The great majority of readers suppose that the device by which Elfleda was substituted for her young mistress, the artifice by which Athelwold obtained the hand of Elfrida, the detection of that artifice, the hunting-party, and the vengeance of the amorous king, are things about which there is no more doubt than about the execution of Anne Boleyn or the slitting of Sir John Coventry's nose. But when we turn to William of Malmesbury, we find that Hume, in his eagerness to relate these pleasant fables, has overlooked one very important circumstance. William does, indeed, tell both the stories; but he gives us distinct notice that he does not warrant their truth, and that they rest on no better authority than that of ballads.*

Such is the way in which these two well-known tales have been handed down. They originally appeared in a poetical form. They found their way from ballads into an old chronicle. The ballads perished; the chronicle remained. A great historian, some centuries after the ballads had been altogether forgotten, consulted the chronicle. He was struck by the lively coloring of these ancient fictions; he transferred them to his pages; and thus we find inserted, as unquestionable facts, in a narrative which is likely to last as long as the English tongue, the inventions of some minstrel whose works were probably never committed to writing, whose name is buried in oblivion, and whose dialect has become obsolete. It must, then, be admitted to be possible, or, rather, highly probable, that the stories of Romulus and Remus,

* "Infamias quas post dicam magis resperserunt cantilenae." Edgar appears to have been most mercilessly treated in the Anglo-Saxon ballads. He was the favorite of the monks; and the monks and minstrels were at deadly feud.

and of the Horatii and Curiatii, may have had a similar origin.

Castilian literature will furnish us with another parallel case. Mariana, the classical historian of Spain, tells the story of the ill-starred marriage which the King Don Alonso brought about between the heirs of Carrion and the two daughters of the Cid. The Cid bestowed a princely dower on his sons-in-law. But the young men were base and proud, cowardly and cruel. They were tried in danger, and found wanting. They fled before the Moors, and once, when a lion broke out of his den, they ran and crouched in an unseemly hiding-place. They knew that they were despised, and took counsel how they might be avenged. They parted from their father-in-law with many signs of love, and set forth on a journey with Doña Elvira and Doña Sol. In a solitary place the bridegrooms seized their brides, stripped them, scourged them, and departed, leaving them for dead. But one of the House of Bivar, suspecting foul play, had followed the travellers in disguise. The ladies were brought back safe to the house of their father. Complaint was made to the king. It was adjudged by the Cortes that the dower given by the Cid should be returned, and that the heirs of Carrion, together with one of their kindred, should do battle against three knights of the party of the Cid. The guilty youths would have declined the combat ; but all their shifts were vain. They were vanquished in the lists and forever disgraced, while their injured wives were sought in marriage by great princes.*

Some Spanish writers have labored to show, by an examination of dates and circumstances, that this story is untrue. Such confutation was surely not needed ; for the narrative is on the face of it a romance. How it found its way into Mariana's history is quite clear. He acknowledges his obligations to the ancient chronicles, and had doubtless before

* Mariana, lib. x. cap. 4.

him the *Crónica del Famoso Cavallero Cid Ruy Diez Campeador*, which had been printed as early as the year 1552. He little suspected that all the most striking passages in this chronicle were copied from a poem of the twelfth century, a poem of which the language and versification had long been obsolete, but which glowed with no common portion of the fire of the *Iliad*. Yet such was the fact. More than a century and a half after the death of Mariana, this venerable ballad, of which one imperfect copy on parchment, four hundred years old, had been preserved at Bivar, was for the first time printed. Then it was found that every interesting circumstance of the story of the heirs of Carrion was derived by the eloquent Jesuit from a song of which he had never heard, and which was composed by a minstrel whose very name had long been forgotten.*

Such, or nearly such, appears to have been the process by which the lost ballad-poetry of Rome was transformed into history. To reverse that process, to transform some portions of early Roman history back into the poetry out of which they were made, is the object of this work.

In the following poems the author speaks, not in his own person, but in the persons of ancient minstrels who know only what a Roman citizen, born three or four hundred years before the Christian era, may be supposed to have known, and who are in no wise above the passions and prejudices of their age and nation. To these imaginary poets must be ascribed some blunders which are so obvious that it is unnecessary to point them out. The real blunder would have been to represent these old poets as deeply versed in general history and studious of chronological accuracy. To them must also be attributed the illiberal sneers at the Greeks, the furi-

---

* See the account which Sanchez gives of the Bivar manuscript in the first volume of the *Coleccion de Poesías Castellanas anteriores al Siglo XV*. Part of the story of the Lords of Carrion, in the poem of the Cid, has been translated by Mr. Frere in a manner above all praise.

ous party-spirit, the contempt for the arts of peace, the love of war for its own sake, the ungenerous exultation over the vanquished, which the reader will sometimes observe. To portray a Roman of the age of Camillus or Curius as superior to national antipathies, as mourning over the devastation and slaughter by which empire and triumphs were to be won, as looking on human suffering with the sympathy of Howard, or as treating conquered enemies with the delicacy of the Black Prince, would be to violate all dramatic propriety. The old Romans had some great virtues—fortitude, temperance, veracity, spirit to resist oppression, respect for legitimate authority, fidelity in the observing of contracts, disinterestedness, ardent patriotism; but Christian charity and chivalrous generosity were alike unknown to them.

It would have been obviously improper to mimic the manner of any particular age or country. Something has been borrowed, however, from our own ballads, and more from Sir Walter Scott, the great restorer of our ballad-poetry. To the *Iliad* still greater obligations are due; and those obligations have been contracted with the less hesitation because there is reason to believe that some of the old Latin minstrels really had recourse to that inexhaustible store of poetical images.

It would have been easy to swell this little volume to a very considerable bulk by appending notes filled with quotations: but to a learned reader such notes are not necessary; for an unlearned reader they would have little interest; and the judgment passed both by the learned and by the unlearned on a work of the imagination will always depend much more on the general character and spirit of such a work than on minute details.

II. CRITICAL COMMENTS ON THE LAYS.

[From a Review by John Stuart Mill.*]

It is with those two great masters of modern ballad-poetry [Scott and Campbell] that Mr. Macaulay's performances are really to be compared, and not with the real ballads or epics of an early age.   The *Lays*, in point of form, are not in the least like the genuine productions of a primitive age or people, and it is no blame to Mr. Macaulay that they are not. He professes imitation of Homer, but we really see no resemblance, except in the nature of some of the incidents and the animation and vigor of the narrative ; and the *Iliad*, after all, is not the original ballad of the Trojan war, but those ballads moulded together and wrought into the forms of a more civilized and cultivated age.   It is difficult to conjecture what the forms of the old Roman ballads may have been, and certain that, whatever they were, they could no more satisfy the æsthetic requirements of modern culture than an ear accustomed to the great organ of Freyburg or Haarlem could relish Orpheus's hurdy-gurdy ; although the airs which Orpheus played, if they could be recovered, might perhaps be executed with great effect on the more perfect instrument.

The forms of Mr. Macaulay's ballad-poetry are essentially modern ; they are those of the romantic and chivalrous, not the classical ages, and even in those they are a reproduction, not of the originals, but of the imitations of Scott.   In this we think he has done well, for Scott's style is as near to that of the ancient ballad as we conceive to be at all compatible with real popular effect on the modern mind.   The difference between the two may be seen by the most cursory comparison of any real old ballad, *Chevy Chase* for instance, with the last canto of *Marmion* or with any of these *Lays*.   Concise-ness is the characteristic of the real ballad, diffuseness of the modern adaptation. The old bard did everything by single touches; Scott and Mr. Macaulay by repetition and accumulation of particulars. They produce all effect by what they *say;* he by what he *suggested*—by what he stimulated the imagination to paint for itself. But then the old ballads were not written for the light reading of tired readers. To do the work in *their* way, they required to be brooded over, or had at least the aid of time and of impassioned recitation. Stories which are to be told to children in the age of eagerness and excitability, or sung in banquet halls to assembled warriors, whose daily ideas and feelings supply a flood of comment ready to gush forth on the slightest hint of the poet, cannot fly too swift and straight to the mark. But Mr. Macaulay wrote only to be read, and by readers for whom it was necessary to do all.

These poems, therefore, are not the worse for being un-Roman in their form; and in their substance they are Roman to a degree which deserves great admiration. . . . We have not been able to detect, in the four poems, one idea or feeling which was not, or might not have been, Roman; while the externals of Roman life, and the feelings characteristic of Rome and of that particular age, are reproduced with great felicity, and without being made unduly predominant over the universal features of human nature and human life.

Independently, therefore, of their value as poems, these compositions are a real service rendered to historical literature; and the author has made this service greater by his prefaces, which will do more than the work of a hundred dissertations in rendering that true conception of early Roman history, the irrefragable establishment of which has made Niebuhr illustrious, familiar to the minds of general readers. This is no trifling matter even in relation to present interests, for there is no estimating the injury which the cause of popular institutions has suffered, and still suffers, from misrepresentation of the early condition of the Roman *plebs* and its noble struggles against its taskmasters. And the study of the manner in which the heroic legends of early Rome grew up as poetry and gradually became history, has important bearings on the general laws of historical evidence and on the many things which, as philosophy advances, are more and more seen to be therewith connected.

[*From Professor Henry Morley's Introduction to the Lays.**]

Macaulay was, perhaps, at his best in his four *Lays of Ancient Rome.* Whatever else he wrote required some qualities of mind other than those which have made all that he wrote popular. The *Lays of Ancient Rome* called into play just those powers which he had in perfection, and required no more. Powers that will ripen only in a meditative mind must remain unripe in the mind of one whose frank and social nature keeps his tongue continually busy. "If any one has anything to say," said Rogers, at one of his breakfasts, "let him say it now. Macaulay's coming." He had only what were called flashes of silence, and a great part of his thinking must have been what came to him in association with the utterance of words. When he was not talking, he was chiefly reading, for he read very much, and his marvellous memory caused what he read to stay by him, good or bad. Most men are able to forget what is not worth keeping in mind, and may thank Heaven that they can. Macaulay, as a young child, went with his mother to pay a call, picked up from the drawing-room table one of Scott's long poems, then just published, read it through while the call lasted, and was able to repeat any quantity of it to his mother after they got home. He enjoyed Scott, and if he had never read Scott's metrical romances the

* From the edition of the *Lays* in "Cassell's National Library" (No. 58), London and New York, 1887.

style of these *Lays* would have shown imitation of some other poet.

But Macaulay caught the swing of Scott's romance measure, made it a little more rhetorical, without loss—some might say rather with increase—of energy, and brought into play his own power of realizing in his mind all that he told. In its expression of that power lies the great and abiding charm of Macaulay's *History*. If it be not whole truth it is as much truth as he saw, and he would see nothing that blurred the outlines of the picture formed in his own mind. Some few truths are so simple and single that they can be stated without any guard or reservation ; the historian who thinks much has to convey to his reader many suggestions of doubt or hesitation. Macaulay took only one view, rejected all that clouded it, accepted all that helped to make it more distinct. He was one of the kindest and truest of men, intensely human ; his one view, whatever it might be, had his own life and feeling in it ; and when set forth in his own clear English, with short sentences that never needed to be lengthened by a qualifying clause—all as fact in broad sunshine about which there did not hang a cloud of doubt— it was, and is, and always will be, delightful reading. It will be thoroughly helpful reading too, for any one who knows the worth of a clear view boldly and honestly expressed, and is able cautiously to use it as aid to the formation of his own opinion. To the untrained reader Macaulay, as historian, is a comfort. That reader, when he inquires, wants always upon every question a plain Yes or No. He dislikes the confusion of doubt. This was disliked also by Macaulay as artist ; and the reader who is only bothered by nice balancings of thought gets from Macaulay always the "plain answer to a plain question," the clear, unhesitating Yes or No which others might consider to be no answer to any question that touches the complexities of human life.

But in a ballad there are no complexities. It is a tale to

be chanted to the people, bound only to be bright and live-ly, with ease in its rhythm, action in every line, and through its whole plan a stirring incident shown clearly from one point of view. It is a tale well told, without any pauses for a nice adjustment of opinion, but appealing simply and directly to a feeling common to us all. It is not concerned with the hard facts of history. Its immediate business may sometimes be to contradict them for the comfort of its hearers.

Thus, in the first of these *Lays*, the old Roman story of three Romans who saved Rome by keeping the bridge over the Tiber against all the force of Porsena, was the ingenious softening of a cruel fact. It turned a day of deep humilia-tion into the bright semblance of a day of glory. For we learn from Tacitus and others that Porsena became abso-lute master of Rome. The Senate of Rome paid homage to him with offering of an ivory throne, a crown, a scep-tre, a triumphal robe ; and he forbade the use of iron by the Romans in forging weapons or armor. The happy time of release from thraldom was long celebrated by a custom of opening auctions with a first bid for " the goods of Por-sena." What did this matter ? The songs of the people were free to suppress a great defeat, and put in its place the myth of a heroic deed ; some small fact usually serv-ing as seed that shall grow and blossom out into a noble tale. A ballad-maker who should stop the course of a pop-ular legend to investigate its origin, and who should be dull enough to include that investigation in his song, would de-serve to be howled to death by the united voices of his countrymen.

Upon this ground, then, Macaulay was a master. His incidents are fully realized. He sees what he sings. When Horatius strikes Astur in the face, the sword's course is fol-lowed " through teeth, and skull, and helmet," till its point stands out a hand-breadth beyond. For its recovery—

> "On Astur's throat Horatius
>   Right firmly pressed his heel,
> And thrice and four times tugged amain,
>   Ere he wrenched out the steel."

The simplicity and vigor of images drawn, like Homer's, from Nature is again in the truest and best spirit of the songs that house themselves among the people. . . .

In the *Lays*, as in the earlier pieces of his ballad-writing, Macaulay liked to paint the stir of battle ; but in *Virginia* there are passages of another strain, and there is tenderness in the description of the main incident. But for *Virginia*, some ungracious reader might say that the *Lays*, being few, are excellent, but that if they were many they might weary by a too close likeness of each to the rest. As it is, the ungracious reader could make no such suggestion. We all read the book with full and natural enjoyment, and we call it perfect in its kind.

[*From Stedman's "Victorian Poets."* *]

Lord Macaulay's *Lays of Ancient Rome* was a literary surprise, but its poetry is the rhythmical outflow of a vigorous and affluent writer, given to splendor of diction and imagery in his flowing prose. He spoke once in verse, and unexpectedly. His themes were legendary, and suited to the author's heroic cast, nor was Latinism ever more poetical than under his thoroughly sympathetic handling. I am aware that the *Lays* are criticised as being stilted and false to the antique, but to me they have a charm, and to almost every healthy young mind are an immediate delight. Where in modern ballad-verse will you find more ringing stanzas, or more impetuous movement and action ? Occasionally we have a noble epithet or image. Within his range—little as one who met him might have surmised it—Macaulay was a poet and

---

* *Victorian Poets*, by Edmund Clarence Stedman (revised ed. Boston, 1887), p. 250.

of the kind which Scott would have been first to honor. *Horatius* and *Virginia* among the Roman lays, and that resonant battle-cry of *Ivry*, have become, it would seem, a lasting portion of English verse.

TIVOLI (THE ANCIENT TIBUR)

MACAULAY'S LAYS OF ANCIENT ROME.

VICTORIA (ROYAL COLLECTION AT MUNICH).

THE RIVER-GOD TIBER.

HORATIUS.

A LAY MADE ABOUT THE YEAR OF THE CITY CCCLX.

I.

LARS PORSENA of Clusium
　By the Nine Gods he swore
That the great house of Tarquin
　Should suffer wrong no more.
By the Nine Gods he swore it,
　And named a trysting-day,
And bade his messengers ride forth,
East and west, and south and north,
　To summon his array.

II.

East and west, and south and north,　10
　The messengers ride fast,
And tower and town and cottage
　Have heard the trumpet's blast.

Shame on the false Etruscan
  Who lingers in his home,
When Porsena of Clusium
  Is on the march for Rome!

III.

The horsemen and the footmen
  Are pouring in amain
From many a stately market-place,   20
  From many a fruitful plain;
From many a lonely hamlet,
  Which, hid by beech and pine,
Like an eagle's nest, hangs on the crest
  Of purple Apennine;

IV.

From lordly Volaterræ,
  Where scowls the far-famed hold
Piled by the hands of giants
  For godlike kings of old;
From sea-girt Populonia,   30
  Whose sentinels descry
Sardinia's snowy mountain-tops
  Fringing the southern sky.;

V.

From the proud mart of Pisæ,
  Queen of the western waves,
Where ride Massilia's triremes
  Heavy with fair-haired slaves;
From where sweet Clanis wanders
  Through corn and vines and flowers;
From where Cortona lifts to heaven   40
  Her diadem of towers.

VI.

Tall are the oaks whose acorns
　　Drop in dark Auser's rill;
Fat are the stags that champ the boughs
　　Of the Ciminian hill;
Beyond all streams Clitumnus
　　Is to the herdsman dear;
Best of all pools the fowler loves
　　The great Volsinian mere.

VII.

But now no stroke of woodman　　50
　　Is heard by Auser's rill;
No hunter tracks the stag's green path
　　Up the Ciminian hill;
Unwatched along Clitumnus
　　Grazes the milk-white steer;
Unharmed the water-fowl may dip
　　In the Volsinian mere.

VIII.

The harvests of Arretium
　　This year old men shall reap;
This year young boys in Umbro　　60
　　Shall plunge the struggling sheep;
And in the vats of Luna
　　This year the must shall foam
Round the white feet of laughing girls
　　Whose sires have marched to Rome.

IX.

There be thirty chosen prophets,
　　The wisest of the land,
Who alway by Lars Porsena
　　Both morn and evening stand;

Evening and morn the Thirty   70
    Have turned the verses o'er,
Traced from the right on linen white
    By mighty seers of yore.

x.

And with one voice the Thirty
    Have their glad answer given:
'Go forth, go forth, Lars Porsena;
    Go forth, beloved of Heaven;
Go, and return in glory
    To Clusium's royal dome,
And hang round Nurscia's altars   80
    The golden shields of Rome.'

xi.

And now hath every city
    Sent up her tale of men;
The foot are fourscore thousand,
    The horse are thousands ten.
Before the gates of Sutrium
    Is met the great array.
A proud man was Lars Porsena
    Upon the trysting-day.

xii.

For all the Etruscan armies   90
    Were ranged beneath his eye,
And many a banished Roman,
    And many a stout ally;
And with a mighty following
    To join the muster came
The Tusculan Mamilius,
    Prince of the Latian name.

XIII.

But by the yellow Tiber
  Was tumult and affright:
From all the spacious champaign   100
  To Rome men took their flight.
A mile around the city
  The throng stopped up the ways;
A fearful sight it was to see
  Through two long nights and days.

XIV.

For aged folk on crutches,
  And women great with child,
And mothers sobbing over babes
  That clung to them and smiled,
And sick men borne in litters   110
  High on the necks of slaves,
And troops of sunburnt husbandmen
  With reaping-hooks and staves,

XV.

And droves of mules and asses
  Laden with skins of wine,
And endless flocks of goats and sheep,
  And endless herds of kine,
And endless trains of wagons
  That creaked beneath the weight
Of corn-sacks and of household goods,   120
  Choked every roaring gate.

XVI.

Now from the rock Tarpeian
  Could the wan burghers spy
The line of blazing villages
  Red in the midnight sky.

The Fathers of the City,
   They sat all night and day,
For every hour some horseman came
   With tidings of dismay.

XVII.

To eastward and to westward   130
   Have spread the Tuscan bands ;
Nor house nor fence nor dovecot
   In Crustumerium stands.
Verbenna down to Ostia
   Hath wasted all the plain ;
Astur hath stormed Janiculum,
   And the stout guards are slain.

XVIII.

I wis, in all the Senate,
   There was no heart so bold
But sore it ached and fast it beat,   140
   When that ill news was told.
Forthwith up rose the Consul,
   Up rose the Fathers all ;
In haste they girded up their gowns,
   And hied them to the wall.

XIX.

They held a council standing
   Before the River Gate ;
Short time was there, ye well may guess,
   For musing or debate.
Out spake the Consul roundly,   150
   'The bridge must straight go down ;
For, since Janiculum is lost,
   Naught else can save the town.'

XX.

Just then a scout came flying,
  All wild with haste and fear :
'To arms ! to arms ! Sir Consul ;
  Lars Porsena is here !'
On the low hills to westward
  The Consul fixed his eye,
And saw the swarthy storm of dust   160
  Rise fast along the sky.

XXI.

And nearer fast, and nearer,
  Doth the red whirlwind come ;
And louder still, and still more loud,
From underneath that rolling cloud,
Is heard the trumpet's war-note proud,
  The trampling and the hum.
And plainly and more plainly
  Now through the gloom appears,
Far to left and far to right,   170
In broken gleams of dark-blue light,
The long array of helmets bright,
  The long array of spears.

XXII.

And plainly and more plainly,
  Above that glimmering line,
Now might ye see the banners
  Of twelve fair cities shine ;
But the banner of proud Clusium
  Was highest of them all,
The terror of the Umbrian,   180
  The terror of the Gaul.

XXIII.

And plainly and more plainly
　　Now might the burghers know,
By port and vest, by horse and crest,
　　Each warlike Lucumo.
There Cilnius of Arretium
　　On his fleet roan was seen;
And Astur of the fourfold shield,
Girt with the brand none else may wield,
Tolumnius with the belt of gold,　　　　　190
And dark Verbenna from the hold
　　By reedy Thrasymene.

XXIV.

Fast by the royal standard,
　　O'erlooking all the war,
Lars Porsena of Clusium
　　Sat in his ivory car.
By the right wheel rode Mamilius,
　　Prince of the Latian name;
And by the left false Sextus,
　　That wrought the deed of shame.　　　　200

XXV.

But when the face of Sextus
　　Was seen among the foes,
A yell that rent the firmament
　　From all the town arose.
On the house-tops was no woman
　　But spat towards him and hissed,
No child but screamed out curses
　　And shook its little fist.

XXVI.

But the Consul's brow was sad,
  And the Consul's speech was low,   210
And darkly looked he at the wall,
  And darkly at the foe.
'Their van will be upon us
  Before the bridge goes down ;
And if they once may win the bridge,
  What hope to save the town ?'

XXVII.

Then out spake brave Horatius,
  The Captain of the Gate :
'To every man upon this earth
  Death cometh soon or late.   220
And how can man die better
  Than facing fearful odds,
For the ashes of his fathers
  And the temples of his gods,

XXVIII.

'And for the tender mother
  Who dandled him to rest,
And for the wife who nurses
  His baby at her breast,
And for the holy maidens
  Who feed the eternal flame,   230
To save them from false Sextus
  That wrought the deed of shame ?

XXIX.

'Hew down the bridge, Sir Consul,
  With all the speed ye may ;
I, with two more to help me,
  Will hold the foe in play.

In yon strait path a thousand
    May well be stopped by three.
Now who will stand on either hand,
    And keep the bridge with me?'   240

XXX.

Then out spake Spurius Lartius;
    A Ramnian proud was he:
'Lo, I will stand at thy right hand,
    And keep the bridge with thee.'
And out spake strong Herminius;
    Of Titian blood was he:
'I will abide on thy left side,
    And keep the bridge with thee.'

XXXI.

'Horatius,' quoth the Consul,
    'As thou sayest, so let it be.'   250
And straight against that great array
    Forth went the dauntless Three.
For Romans in Rome's quarrel
    Spared neither land nor gold,
Nor son nor wife, nor limb nor life,
    In the brave days of old.

XXXII.

Then none was for a party;
    Then all were for the State;
Then the great man helped the poor,
    And the poor man loved the great: 260
Then lands were fairly portioned;
    Then spoils were fairly sold;
The Romans were like brothers
    In the brave days of old.

XXXIII.

Now Roman is to Roman
   More hateful than a foe;
And the Tribunes beard the high,
   And the Fathers grind the low.
As we wax hot in faction,
   In battle we wax cold;   270
Wherefore men fight not as they fought
   In the brave days of old.

XXXIV.

Now while the Three were tightening
   Their harness on their backs,
The Consul was the foremost man
   To take in hand an axe;
And Fathers mixed with Commons
   Seized hatchet, bar, and crow,
And smote upon the planks above,
   And loosed the props below.   280

XXXV.

Meanwhile the Tuscan army,
   Right glorious to behold,
Come flashing back the noonday light,
Rank behind rank, like surges bright
   Of a broad sea of gold.
Four hundred trumpets sounded
   A peal of warlike glee,
As that great host, with measured tread,
And spears advanced, and ensigns spread,
Rolled slowly towards the bridge's head,   290
   Where stood the dauntless Three.

4

XXXVI.

The Three stood calm and silent,
    And looked upon the foes,
And a great shout of laughter
    From all the vanguard rose;
And forth three chiefs came spurring
    Before that deep array:
To earth they sprang, their swords they drew,
And lifted high their shields, and flew
    To win the narrow way: 300

XXXVII.

Aunus from green Tifernum,
    Lord of the Hill of Vines;
And Seius, whose eight hundred slaves
    Sicken in Ilva's mines;
And Picus, long to Clusium
    Vassal in peace and war,
Who led to fight his Umbrian powers
From that gray crag where, girt with towers,
The fortress of Nequinum lowers
    O'er the pale waves of Nar.   310

XXXVIII.

Stout Lartius hurled down Aunus
    Into the stream beneath;
Herminius struck at Seius,
    And clove him to the teeth;
At Picus brave Horatius
    Darted one fiery thrust,
And the proud Umbrian's gilded arms
    Clashed in the bloody dust.

XXXIX.

Then Ocnus of Falerii
 Rushed on the Roman Three ;   320
And Lausulus of Urgo,
 The rover of the sea ;
And Aruns of Volsinium,
 Who slew the great wild boar,
The great wild boar that had his den
Amidst the reeds of Cosa's fen,
And wasted fields and slaughtered men
 Along Albinia's shore.

XL.

Herminius smote down Aruns ;
 Lartius laid Ocnus low ;   330
Right to the heart of Lausulus
 Horatius sent a blow.
'Lie there,' he cried, 'fell pirate !
 No more, aghast and pale,
From Ostia's walls the crowd shall mark
The track of thy destroying bark.
No more Campania's hinds shall fly
To woods and caverns when they spy
 Thy thrice accursed sail.'

XLI.

But now no sound of laughter   340
 Was heard among the foes ;
A wild and wrathful clamor
 From all the vanguard rose.
Six spears' length from the entrance
 Halted that deep array,
And for a space no man came forth
 To win the narrow way.

XLII.

But hark! the cry is Astur;
   And lo! the ranks divide,
And the great Lord of Luna   350
   Comes with his stately stride.
Upon his ample shoulders
   Clangs loud the fourfold shield,
And in his hand he shakes the brand
   Which none but he can wield.

XLIII.

He smiled on those bold Romans
   A smile serene and high;
He eyed the flinching Tuscans,
   And scorn was in his eye.
Quoth he, 'The she-wolf's litter   360
   Stand savagely at bay;
But will ye dare to follow,
   If Astur clears the way?'

XLIV.

Then, whirling up his broadsword
   With both hands to the height,
He rushed against Horatius,
   And smote with all his might.
With shield and blade Horatius
   Right deftly turned the blow.
The blow, though turned, came yet too nigh; 370
It missed his helm, but gashed his thigh:
The Tuscans raised a joyful cry
   To see the red blood flow.

XLV.

He reeled and on Herminius
   He leaned one breathing-space,
Then, like a wild cat mad with wounds,
   Sprang right at Astur's face.
Through teeth and skull and helmet
   So fierce a thrust he sped,
The good sword stood a hand-breadth out   380
   Behind the Tuscan's head.

XLVI.

And the great Lord of Luna
   Fell at that deadly stroke,
As falls on Mount Alvernus
   A thunder-smitten oak.
Far o'er the crashing forest
   The giant arms lie spread;
And the pale augurs, muttering low,
   Gaze on the blasted head.

XLVII.

On Astur's throat Horatius   390
   Right firmly pressed his heel,
And thrice and four times tugged amain
   Ere he wrenched out the steel.
'And see,' he cried, 'the welcome,
   Fair guests, that waits you here!
What noble Lucumo comes next
   To taste our Roman cheer?'

XLVIII.

But at his haughty challenge
   A sullen murmur ran,
Mingled of wrath and shame and dread,   400
   Along that glittering van.

There lacked not men of prowess,
  Nor men of lordly race;
For all Etruria's noblest
  Were round the fatal place.

XLIX.

But all Etruria's noblest
  Felt their hearts sink to see
On the earth the bloody corpses,
  In the path the dauntless Three;
And, from the ghastly entrance   410
  Where those bold Romans stood,
All shrank, like boys who, unaware,
Ranging the woods to start a hare,
Come to the mouth of the dark lair
Where, growling low, a fierce old bear
  Lies amidst bones and blood.

L.

Was none who would be foremost
  To lead such dire attack;
But those behind cried 'Forward!'
  And those before cried 'Back!'   420
And backward now and forward
  Wavers the deep array;
And on the tossing sea of steel
To and fro the standards reel,
And the victorious trumpet-peal
  Dies fitfully away.

LI.

Yet one man for one moment
  Strode out before the crowd;
Well known was he to all the Three,
  And they gave him greeting loud.   430

'Now welcome, welcome, Sextus!
  Now welcome to thy home!
Why dost thou stay and turn away?
  Here lies the road to Rome.'

LII.

Thrice looked he at the city,
  Thrice looked he at the dead;
And thrice came on in fury,
  And thrice turned back in dread;
And, white with fear and hatred,
  Scowled at the narrow way   440
Where, wallowing in a pool of blood,
  The bravest Tuscans lay.

LIII.

But meanwhile axe and lever
  Have manfully been plied,
And now the bridge hangs tottering
  Above the boiling tide.
'Come back, come back, Horatius!'
  Loud cried the Fathers all.
'Back, Lartius! back, Herminius!
  Back, ere the ruin fall!'   458

LIV.

Back darted Spurius Lartius,
  Herminius darted back;
And, as they passed, beneath their feet
  They felt the timbers crack.
But when they turned their faces,
  And on the farther shore
Saw brave Horatius stand alone,
  They would have crossed once more.

LV.

But with a crash like thunder
    Fell every loosened beam,   460
And, like a dam, the mighty wreck
    Lay right athwart the stream;
And a long shout of triumph
    Rose from the walls of Rome,
As to the highest turret-tops
    Was splashed the yellow foam.

LVI.

And, like a horse unbroken
    When first he feels the rein,
The furious river struggled hard,
    And tossed his tawny mane,   470
And burst the curb and bounded,
    Rejoicing to be free,
And, whirling down in fierce career
Battlement and plank and pier,
    Rushed headlong to the sea.

LVII.

Alone stood brave Horatius
    But constant still in mind,
Thrice thirty thousand foes before
    And the broad flood behind.
'Down with him!' cried false Sextus,   480
    With a smile on his pale face.
'Now yield thee,' cried Lars Porsena,
    'Now yield thee to our grace.'

LVIII.

Round turned he, as not deigning
    Those craven ranks to see;
Naught spake he to Lars Porsena,
    To Sextus naught spake he;

But he saw on Palatinus
   The white porch of his home,
And he spake to the noble river   490
   That rolls by the towers of Rome :

LIX.

'O Tiber ! father Tiber !
   To whom the Romans pray,
A Roman's life, a Roman's arms,
   Take thou in charge this day !'
So he spake, and speaking sheathed
   The good sword by his side,
And with his harness on his back
   Plunged headlong in the tide.

LX.

No sound of joy or sorrow   500
   Was heard from either bank,
But friends and foes in dumb surprise,
With parted lips and straining eyes,
   Stood gazing where he sank ;
And when above the surges
   They saw his crest appear,
All Rome sent forth a rapturous cry,
And even the ranks of Tuscany
   Could scarce forbear to cheer.

LXI.

But fiercely ran the current,   510
   Swollen high by months of rain ;
And fast his blood was flowing,
   And he was sore in pain,
And heavy with his armor,
   And spent with changing blows :
And oft they thought him sinking,
   But still again he rose.

LXII.

Never, I ween, did swimmer,
  In such an evil case,
Struggle through such a raging flood   520
  Safe to the landing-place;
But his limbs were borne up bravely
  By the brave heart within,
And our good father Tiber
  Bare bravely up his chin.

LXIII.

' Curse on him !' quoth false Sextus;
  ' Will not the villain drown?
But for this stay, ere close of day
  We should have sacked the town !'
' Heaven help him !' quoth Lars Porsena,   530
  ' And bring him safe to shore;
For such a gallant feat of arms
  Was never seen before.'

LXIV.

And now he feels the bottom;
  Now on dry earth he stands;
Now round him throng the Fathers
  To press his gory hands;
And now, with shouts and clapping
  And noise of weeping loud,
He enters through the River Gate,   540
  Borne by the joyous crowd.

LXV.

They gave him of the corn-land,
  That was of public right,
As much as two strong oxen
  Could plough from morn till night;

And they made a molten image
    And set it up on high,
And there it stands unto this day
    To witness if I lie.

LXVI.

It stands in the Comitium,   550
    Plain for all folk to see,
Horatius in his harness
    Halting upon one knee ;
And underneath is written,
    In letters all of gold,
How valiantly he kept the bridge
    In the brave days of old.

LXVII.

And still his name sounds stirring
    Unto the men of Rome,
As the trumpet-blast that cries to them   560
    To charge the Volscian home ;
And wives still pray to Juno
    For boys with hearts as bold
As his who kept the bridge so well
    In the brave days of old.

LXVIII.

And in the nights of winter,
    When the cold north winds blow,
And the long howling of the wolves
    Is heard amidst the snow ;
When round the lonely cottage   570
    Roars loud the tempest's din,
And the good logs of Algidus
    Roar louder yet within ;

LXIX.

When the oldest cask is opened,
  And the largest lamp is lit;
When the chestnuts glow in the embers,
  And the kid turns on the spit;
When young and old in circle
  Around the firebrands close;
When the girls are weaving baskets,   580
  And the lads are shaping bows;

LXX.

When the goodman mends his armor,
  And trims his helmet's plume;
When the goodwife's shuttle merrily
  Goes flashing through the loom;
With weeping and with laughter
  Still is the story told,
How well Horatius kept the bridge
  In the brave days of old.

ROMAN VICTORY.

THE BATTLE OF THE LAKE REGILLUS.

A LAY SUNG AT THE FEAST OF CASTOR AND POLLUX
ON THE IDES OF QUINTILIS, IN THE YEAR OF THE
CITY CCCCLI.

I.

Ho, trumpets, sound a war-note!
  Ho, lictors, clear the way!
The knights will ride, in all their pride,
  Along the streets to-day.
To-day the doors and windows
  Are hung with garlands all,
From Castor in the Forum
  To Mars without the wall.

Each knight is robed in purple,
    With olive each is crowned ;   10
A gallant war-horse under each
    Paws haughtily the ground.
While flows the Yellow River,
    While stands the Sacred Hill,
The proud ides of Quintilis
    Shall have such honor still.
Gay are the Martian calends,
    December's nones are gay ;
But the proud ides, when the squadron rides,
    Shall be Rome's whitest day.   20

II.

Unto the Great Twin Brethren
    We keep this solemn feast.
Swift, swift, the Great Twin Brethren
    Came spurring from the east.
They came o'er wild Parthenius
    Tossing in waves of pine,
O'er Cirrha's dome, o'er Adria's foam,
    O'er purple Apennine,
From where with flutes and dances
    Their ancient mansion rings   30
In lordly Lacedæmon,
    The city of two kings,
To where, by Lake Regillus,
    Under the Porcian height,
All in the lands of Tusculum,
    Was fought the glorious fight.

III.

Now on the place of slaughter
    Are cots and sheepfolds seen,

And rows of vines, and fields of wheat,
  And apple-orchards green ;   40
The swine crush the big acorns
  That fall from Corne's oaks ;
Upon the turf by the Fair Fount
  The reaper's pottage smokes.
The fisher baits his angle,
  The hunter twangs his bow ;
Little they think on those strong limbs
  That moulder deep below.
Little they think how sternly
  That day the trumpets pealed ;   50
How in the slippery swamp of blood
  Warrior and war-horse reeled ;
How wolves came with fierce gallop,
  And crows on eager wings,
To tear the flesh of captains,
  And peck the eyes of kings ;
How thick the dead lay scattered
  Under the Porcian height ;
How through the gates of Tusculum
  Raved the wild stream of flight ;   60
And how the Lake Regillus
  Bubbled with crimson foam,
What time the Thirty Cities
  Came forth to war with Rome.

IV.

But, Roman, when thou standest
  Upon that holy ground,
Look thou with heed on the dark rock
  That girds the dark lake round.
So shalt thou see a hoof-mark
  Stamped deep into the flint ;   70

It was no hoof of mortal steed
　　That made so strange a dint.
There to the Great Twin Brethren
　　Vow thou thy vows, and pray
That they, in tempest and in fight,
　　Will keep thy head alway.

V.

Since last the Great Twin Brethren
　　Of mortal eyes were seen,
Have years gone by an hundred
　　And fourscore and thirteen.　　　　80
That summer a Virginius
　　Was Consul first in place;
The second was stout Aulus,
　　Of the Posthumian race.
The herald of the Latines
　　From Gabii came in state;
The herald of the Latines
　　Passed through Rome's Eastern Gate;
The herald of the Latines
　　Did in our Forum stand;　　　　90
And there he did his office,
　　A sceptre in his hand:

VI.

' Hear, Senators and people
　　Of the good town of Rome!
The Thirty Cities charge you
　　To bring the Tarquins home;
And if ye still be stubborn
　　To work the Tarquins wrong,
The Thirty Cities warn you,
　　Look that your walls be strong.'　　　　100

VII.

Then spake the Consul Aulus—
    He spake a bitter jest—
'Once the jays sent a message
    Unto the eagle's nest :
Now yield thou up thine eyry
    Unto the carrion-kite,
Or come forth valiantly and face
    The jays in deadly fight.—
Forth looked in wrath the eagle ;
    And carrion-kite and jay,   110
Soon as they saw his beak and claw,
    Fled screaming far away.'

VIII.

The herald of the Latines
    Hath hied him back in state ;
The Fathers of the city
    Are met in high debate.
Then spake the elder Consul,
    An ancient man and wise :
'Now hearken, Conscript Fathers,
    To that which I advise.   120
In seasons of great peril
    'T is good that one bear sway ;
Then choose we a Dictator,
    Whom all men shall obey.
Camerium knows how deeply
    The sword of Aulus bites,
And all our city calls him
    The man of seventy fights.
Then let him be Dictator
    For six months, and no more,   130
And have a Master of the Knights
    And axes twenty-four.'

5

IX.

So Aulus was Dictator,
　　The man of seventy fights ;
He made Æbutius Elva
　　His Master of the Knights.
On the third morn thereafter,
　　At dawning of the day,
Did Aulus and Æbutius
　　Set forth with their array.　　　　140
Sempronius Atratinus
　　Was left in charge at home,
With boys and with gray-headed men
　　To keep the walls of Rome.
Hard by the Lake Regillus
　　Our camp was pitched at night ;
Eastward a mile the Latines lay,
　　Under the Porcian height.
Far over hill and valley
　　Their mighty host was spread,　　　150
And with their thousand watch-fires
　　The midnight sky was red.

X.

Up rose the golden morning
　　Over the Porcian height,
The proud ides of Quintilis
　　Marked evermore with white.
Not without secret trouble
　　Our bravest saw the foes ;
For girt by threescore thousand spears
　　The thirty standards rose.　　　　160
From every warlike city
　　That boasts the Latian name,
Foredoomed to dogs and vultures,
　　That gallant army came :

From Setia's purple vineyards,
   From Norba's ancient wall,
From the white streets of Tusculum,
   The proudest town of all ;
From where the Witch's Fortress
   O'erhangs the dark-blue seas ;   170
From the still glassy lake that sleeps
   Beneath Aricia's trees—
Those trees in whose dim shadow
   The ghastly priest doth reign,
The priest who slew the slayer,
   And shall himself be slain ;
From the drear banks of Ufens,
   Where flights of marsh-fowl play,
And buffaloes lie wallowing
   Through the hot summer's day ;   180
From the gigantic watch-towers,
   No work of earthly men,
Whence Cora's sentinels o'erlook
   The never-ending fen ;
From the Laurentian jungle,
   The wild hog's reedy home ;
From the green steeps whence Anio leaps
   In floods of snow-white foam.

XI.

Aricia, Cora, Norba,
   Velitræ, with the might   190
Of Setia and of Tusculum,
   Were marshalled on the right.
Their leader was Mamilius,
   Prince of the Latian name :
Upon his head a helmet
   Of red gold shone like flame ;

High on a gallant charger
  Of dark-gray hue he rode ;
Over his gilded armor
  A vest of purple flowed,   200
Woven in the land of sunrise
  By Syria's dark-browed daughters,
And by the sails of Carthage brought
  Far o'er the southern waters.

XII.

Lavinium and Laurentum
  Had on the left their post,
With all the banners of the marsh,
  And banners of the coast.
Their leader was false Sextus,
  That wrought the deed of shame ;   210
With restless pace and haggard face
  To his last field he came.
Men said he saw strange visions
  Which none beside might see,
And that strange sounds were in his ears
  Which none might hear but he.
A woman fair and stately,
  But pale as are the dead,
Oft through the watches of the night
  Sat spinning by his bed ;   220
And as she plied the distaff,
  In a sweet voice and low,
She sang of great old houses
  And fights fought long ago.
So spun she and so sang she
  Until the east was gray,
Then pointed to her bleeding breast,
  And shrieked, and fled away.

XIII.

But in the centre thickest
　　Were ranged the shields of foes,　　230
And from the centre loudest
　　The cry of battle rose.
There Tibur marched, and Pedum,
　　Beneath proud Tarquin's rule,
And Ferentinum of the rock,
　　And Gabii of the pool.
There rode the Volscian succors;
　　There, in a dark stern ring,
The Roman exiles gathered close
　　Around the ancient king.　　240
Though white as Mount Soracte
　　When winter nights are long
His beard flowed down o'er mail and belt,
　　His heart and hand were strong;
Under his hoary eyebrows
　　Still flashed forth quenchless rage;
And if the lance shook in his gripe,
　　'T was more with hate than age.
Close at his side was Titus
　　On an Apulian steed—　　250
Titus, the youngest Tarquin,
　　Too good for such a breed.

XIV.

Now on each side the leaders
　　Gave signal for the charge;
And on each side the footmen
　　Strode on with lance and targe;
And on each side the horsemen
　　Struck their spurs deep in gore,

And front to front the armies
   Met with a mighty roar ;   260
And under that great battle
   The earth with blood was red ;
And, like the Pomptine fog at morn,
   The dust hung overhead ;
And louder still and louder
   Rose from the darkened field
The braying of the war-horns,
   The clang of sword and shield,
The rush of squadrons sweeping
   Like whirlwinds o'er the plain,   270
The shouting of the slayers,
   And screeching of the slain.

XV.

False Sextus rode out foremost,
   His look was high and bold ;
His corselet was of bison's hide,
   Plated with steel and gold.
As glares the famished eagle
   From the Digentian rock
On a choice lamb that bounds alone
   Before Bandusia's flock,   280
Herminius glared on Sextus
   And came with eagle speed,
Herminius on black Auster,
   Brave champion on brave steed ;
In his right hand the broadsword
   That kept the bridge so well,
And on his helm the crown he won
   When proud Fidenæ fell.
Woe to the maid whose lover
   Shall cross his path to-day !   290

False Sextus saw and trembled,
　And turned and fled away.
As turns, as flies, the woodman
　In the Calabrian brake,
When through the reeds gleams the round eye
　Of that fell speckled snake,
So turned, so fled, false Sextus,
　And hid him in the rear,
Behind the dark Lavinian ranks
　Bristling with crest and spear.　　　　300

XVI.

But far to north Æbutius,
　The Master of the Knights,
Gave Tubero of Norba
　To feed the Porcian kites.
Next under those red horse-hoofs
　Flaccus of Setia lay;
Better had he been pruning
　Among his elms that day.
Mamilius saw the slaughter,
　And tossed his golden crest,　　　　310
And towards the Master of the Knights
　Through the thick battle pressed.
Æbutius smote Mamilius
　So fiercely on the shield
That the great lord of Tusculum
　Well-nigh rolled on the field.
Mamilius smote Æbutius,
　With a good aim and true,
Just where the neck and shoulder join,
　And pierced him through and through;　　320
And brave Æbutius Elva
　Fell swooning to the ground,

But a thick wall of bucklers
    Encompassed him around.
His clients from the battle
    Bare him some little space,
And filled a helm from the dark lake
    And bathed his brow and face;
And when at last he opened
    His swimming eyes to light,   330
Men say the earliest word he spake
    Was, 'Friends, how goes the fight?'

XVII.

But meanwhile in the centre
    Great deeds of arms were wrought;
There Aulus the Dictator
    And there Valerius fought.
Aulus with his good broadsword
    A bloody passage cleared
To where, amidst the thickest foes,
    He saw the long white beard.   340
Flat lighted that good broadsword
    Upon proud Tarquin's head.
He dropped the lance, he dropped the reins;
    He fell as fall the dead.
Down Aulus springs to slay him,
    With eyes like coals of fire;
But faster Titus hath sprung down,
    And hath bestrode his sire.
Latian captains, Roman knights,
    Fast down to earth they spring,   350
And hand to hand they fight on foot
    Around the ancient king.
First Titus gave tall Cæso
    A death-wound in the face—

Tall Cæso was the bravest man
　Of the brave Fabian race;
Aulus slew Rex of Gabii,
　The priest of Juno's shrine;
Valerius smote down Julius,
　Of Rome's great Julian line—　　　　360
Julius, who left his mansion
　High on the Velian hill,
And through all turns of weal and woe
　Followed proud Tarquin still.
Now right across proud Tarquin
　A corpse was Julius laid;
And Titus groaned with rage and grief,
　And at Valerius made.
Valerius struck at Titus,
　And lopped off half his crest;　　　　370
But Titus stabbed Valerius
　A span deep in the breast.
Like a mast snapped by the tempest,
　Valerius reeled and fell.
Ah! woe is me for the good house
　That loves the people well!
Then shouted loud the Latines,
　And with one rush they bore
The struggling Romans backward
　Three lances' length and more;　　　　380
And up they took proud Tarquin,
　And laid him on a shield,
And four strong yeomen bare him,
　Still senseless, from the field.

XVIII.

But fiercer grew the fighting
　Around Valerius dead;

For Titus dragged him by the foot,
  And Aulus by the head.
'On, Latines, on!' quoth Titus,
  'See how the rebels fly!'   390
'Romans, stand firm!' quoth Aulus,
  'And win this fight or die!
They must not give Valerius
  To raven and to kite;
For aye Valerius loathed the wrong,
  And aye upheld the right;
And for your wives and babies
  In the front rank he fell.
Now play the men for the good house
  That loves the people well!'   400

XIX.

Then tenfold round the body
  The roar of battle .rose,
Like the roar of a burning forest
  When a strong north wind blows.
Now backward and now forward
  Rocked furiously the fray,
Till none could see Valerius,
  And none wist where he lay.
For shivered arms and ensigns
  Were heaped there in a mound,   410
And corpses stiff and dying men
  That writhed and gnawed the ground,
And wounded horses kicking
  And snorting purple foam;
Right well did such a couch befit
  A Consular of Rome.

XX.

But north looked the Dictator;
  North looked he long and hard,

And spake to Caius Cossus,
　　The Captain of his Guard :   420
'Caius, of all the Romans,
　　Thou hast the keenest sight ;
Say, what through yonder storm of dust
　　Comes from the Latian right?'

XXI.

Then answered Caius Cossus :
　　' I see an evil sight ;
The banner of proud Tusculum
　　Comes from the Latian right.
I see the plumed horsemen ;
　　And far before the rest   430
I see the dark-gray charger,
　　I see the purple vest ;
I see the golden helmet
　　That shines far off like flame ;
So ever rides Mamilius,
　　Prince of the Latian name.'

XXII.

'Now hearken, Caius Cossus :
　　Spring on thy horse's back ;
Ride as the wolves of Apennine
　　Were all upon thy track ;   440
Haste to our southward battle,
　　And never draw thy rein
Until thou find Herminius,
　　And bid him come amain.'

XXIII.

So Aulus spake, and turned him
　　Again to that fierce strife ;
And Caius Cossus mounted,
　　And rode for death and life.

Loud clanged beneath his horse-hoofs
  The helmets of the dead,   450
And many a curdling pool of blood
  Splashed him from heel to head.
So came he far to southward,
  Where fought the Roman host
Against the banners of the marsh
  And banners of the coast.
Like corn before the sickle
  The stout Lavinians fell,
Beneath the edge of the true sword
  That kept the bridge so well.   460

XXIV.

'Herminius, Aulus greets thee;
  He bids thee come with speed
To help our central battle,
  For sore is there our need.
There wars the youngest Tarquin,
  And there the Crest of Flame,
The Tusculan Mamilius,
  Prince of the Latian name.
Valerius hath fallen fighting
  In front of our array,   470
And Aulus of the seventy fields
  Alone upholds the day.'

XXV.

Herminius beat his bosom,
  But never a word he spake.
He clapped his hand on Auster's mane,
  He gave the reins a shake;
Away, away, went Auster,
  Like an arrow from the bow—

Black Auster was the fleetest steed
  From Aufidus to Po.   480

XXVI.

Right glad were all the Romans
  Who, in that hour of dread,
Against great odds bare up the war
  Around Valerius dead,
When from the south the cheering
  Rose with a mighty swell :
' Herminius comes, Herminius,
  Who kept the bridge so well !'

XXVII.

Mamilius spied Herminius,
  And dashed across the way :   490
' Herminius, I have sought thee
  Through many a bloody day.
One of us two, Herminius,
  Shall never more go home.
I will lay on for Tusculum,
  And lay thou on for Rome !'

XXVIII.

All round them paused the battle,
  While met in mortal fray
The Roman and the Tusculan,
  The horses black and gray.   500
Herminius smote Mamilius
  Through breastplate and through breast,
And fast flowed out the purple blood
  Over the purple vest.
Mamilius smote Herminius
  Through head-piece and through head ;
And side by side those chiefs of pride
  Together fell down dead.

Down fell they dead together
   In a great lake of gore ;   510
And still stood all who saw them fall
   While men might count a score.

XXIX.

Fast, fast, with heels wild spurning,
   The dark-gray charger fled ;
He burst through ranks of fighting-men,
   He sprang o'er heaps of dead.
His bridle far outstreaming,
   His flanks all blood and foam,
He sought the southern mountains,
   The mountains of his home.   520
The pass was steep and rugged,
   The wolves they howled and whined ;
But he ran like a whirlwind up the pass,
   And he left the wolves behind.
Through many a startled hamlet
   Thundered his flying feet ;
He rushed through the gate of Tusculum,
   He rushed up the long white street ;
He rushed by tower and temple,
   And paused not from his race   530
Till he stood before his master's door
   In the stately market-place.
And straightway round him gathered
   A pale and trembling crowd ;
And, when they knew him, cries of rage
   Brake forth, and wailing loud ;
And women rent their tresses
   For their great prince's fall ;
And old men girt on their old swords,
   And went to man the wall.   540

XXX.

But, like a graven image,
   Black Auster kept his place,
And ever wistfully he looked
   Into his master's face.
The raven mane that daily,
   With pats and fond caresses,
The young Herminia washed and combed,
   And twined in even tresses,
And decked with colored ribbons
   From her own gay attire,   550
Hung sadly o'er her father's corpse
   In carnage and in mire.
Forth with a shout sprang Titus,
   And seized black Auster's rein.
Then Aulus sware a fearful oath,
   And ran at him amain:
'The furies of thy brother
   With me and mine abide,
If one of your accursed house
   Upon black Auster ride!'   560
As on an Alpine watch-tower
   From heaven comes down the flame,
Full on the neck of Titus
   The blade of Aulus came;
And out the red blood spouted
   In a wide arch and tall,
As spouts a fountain in the court
   Of some rich Capuan's hall.
The knees of all the Latines
   Were loosened with dismay   570
When dead, on dead Herminius,
   The bravest Tarquin lay.

XXXI.

And Aulus the Dictator
  Stroked Auster's raven mane,
With heed he looked unto the girths,
  With heed unto the rein:
'Now bear me well, black Auster,
  Into yon thick array,
And thou and I will have revenge
  For thy good lord this day.'   580

XXXII.

So spake he, and was buckling
  Tighter black Auster's band,
When he was aware of a princely pair
  That rode at his right hand.
So like they were, no mortal
  Might one from other know;
White as snow their armor was,
  Their steeds were white as snow.
Never on earthly anvil
  Did such rare armor gleam,   590
And never did such gallant steeds
  Drink of an earthly stream.

XXXIII.

And all who saw them trembled,
  And pale grew every cheek;
And Aulus the Dictator
  Scarce gathered voice to speak:
'Say by what name men call you?
  What city is your home?
And wherefore ride ye in such guise
  Before the ranks of Rome?'   600

XXXIV.

'By many names men call us,
  In many lands we dwell:
Well Samothracia knows us,
  Cyrene knows us well;
Our house in gay Tarentum
  Is hung each morn with flowers;
High o'er the masts of Syracuse
  Our marble portal towers;
But by the proud Eurotas
  Is our dear native home;   610
And for the right we come to fight
  Before the ranks of Rome.'

XXXV.

So answered those strange horsemen,
  And each couched low his spear;
And forthwith all the ranks of Rome
  Were bold and of good cheer;
And on the thirty armies
  Came wonder and affright,
And Ardea wavered on the left,
  And Cora on the right.   620
'Rome to the charge!' cried Aulus;
  'The foe begins to yield!
Charge for the hearth of Vesta!
  Charge for the Golden Shield!
Let no man stop to plunder,
  But slay, and slay, and slay;
The gods, who live forever,
  Are on our side to-day.'

6

XXXVI.

Then the fierce trumpet-flourish
  From earth to heaven arose;   630
The kites know well the long stern swell
  That bids the Romans close.
Then the good sword of Aulus
  Was lifted up to slay;
Then, like a crag down Apennine,
  Rushed Auster through the fray.
But under those strange horsemen
  Still thicker lay the slain,
And after those strange horses
  Black Auster toiled in vain.   640
Behind them Rome's long battle
  Came rolling on the foe,
Ensigns dancing wild above,
  Blades all in line below.
So comes the Po in flood-time
  Upon the Celtic plain;
So comes the squall, blacker than night,
  Upon the Adrian main.
Now, by our sire Quirinus,
  It was a goodly sight   650
To see the thirty standards
  Swept down the tide of flight!
So flies the spray of Adria
  When the black squall doth blow;
So corn-sheaves in the flood-time
  Spin down the whirling Po.
False Sextus to the mountains
  Turned first his horse's head;
And fast fled Ferentinum,
  And fast Lanuvium fled.   660

The horsemen of Nomentum
  Spurred hard out of the fray ;
The footmen of Velitræ
  Threw shield and spear away.
And underfoot was trampled,
  Amidst the mud and gore,
The banner of proud Tusculum,
  That never stooped before ;
And down went Flavius Faustus,
  Who led his stately ranks   670
From where the apple-blossoms wave
  On Anio's echoing banks ;
And Tullus of Arpinum,
  Chief of the Volscian aids,
And Metius with the long fair curls,
  The love of Anxur's maids ;
And the white head of Vulso,
  The great Arician seer ;
And Nepos of Laurentum,
  The hunter of the deer ;   680
And in the back false Sextus
  Felt the good Roman steel,
And wriggling in the dust he died,
  Like a worm beneath the wheel ;
And fliers and pursuers
  Were mingled in a mass ;
And far away the battle
  Went roaring through the pass.

XXXVII.

Sempronius Atratinus
  Sat in the Eastern Gate,   690
Beside him were three Fathers,
  Each in his chair of state—

Fabius, whose nine stout grandsons
  That day were in the field,
And Manlius, eldest of the Twelve
  Who keep the Golden Shield ;
And Sergius, the High Pontiff,
  For wisdom far renowned—
In all Etruria's colleges
  Was no such pontiff found.   700
And all around the portal,
  And high above the wall,
Stood a great throng of people,
  But sad and silent all ;
Young lads and stooping elders
  That might not bear the mail,
Matrons with lips that quivered,
  And maids with faces pale.
Since the first gleam of daylight,
  Sempronius had not ceased   710
To listen for the rushing
  Of horse-hoofs from the east.
The mist of eve was rising,
  The sun was hastening down,
When he was aware of a princely pair
  Fast pricking towards the town.
So like they were, man never
  Saw twins so like before ;
Red with gore their armor was,
  Their steeds were red with gore.   720

XXXVIII.

' Hail to the great Asylum !
  Hail to the hill-tops seven !
Hail to the fire that burns for aye,
  And the shield that fell from heaven !

This day, by Lake Regillus,
   Under the Porcian height,
All in the lands of Tusculum
   Was fought a glorious fight.
To-morrow your Dictator
   Shall bring in triumph home   730
The spoils of thirty cities
   To deck the shrines of Rome!'

XXXIX.

Then burst from that great concourse
   A shout that shook the towers,
And some ran north, and some ran south,
   Crying, 'The day is ours!'
But on rode these strange horsemen
   With slow and lordly pace,
And none who saw their bearing
   Durst ask their name or race.   740
On rode they to the Forum,
   While laurel boughs and flowers,
From house-tops and from windows,
   Fell on their crests in showers.
When they drew nigh to Vesta,
   They vaulted down amain,
And washed their horses in the well
   That springs by Vesta's fane.
And straight again they mounted,
   And rode to Vesta's door;   750
Then, like a blast, away they passed,
   And no man saw them more.

XL.

And all the people trembled,
   And pale grew every cheek;

And Sergius the High Pontiff
  Alone found voice to speak :
'The gods who live forever
  Have fought for Rome to-day!
These be the Great Twin Brethren
  To whom the Dorians pray.   760
Back comes the chief in triumph
  Who in the hour of fight
Hath seen the Great Twin Brethren
  In harness on his right.
Safe comes the ship to haven,
  Through billows and through gales,
If once the Great Twin Brethren
  Sit shining on the sails.
Wherefore they washed their horses
  In Vesta's holy well,   770
Wherefore they rode to Vesta's door,
  I know, but may not tell.
Here, hard by Vesta's temple,
  Build we a stately dome
Unto the Great Twin Brethren
  Who fought so well for Rome.
And when the months returning
  Bring back this day of fight,
The proud ides of Quintilis,
  Marked evermore with white,   780
Unto the Great Twin Brethren
  Let all the people throng,
With chaplets and with offerings,
  With music and with song ;
And let the doors and windows
  Be hung with garlands all,
And let the knights be summoned
  To Mars without the wall ;

Thence let them ride in purple
  With joyous trumpet-sound,
Each mounted on his war-horse
  And each with olive crowned,
And pass in solemn order
  Before the sacred dome
Where dwell the Great Twin Brethren
  Who fought so well for Rome.'

790

ROMAN SOLDIERS (FROM COLUMN OF TRAJAN).

THE FORUM, BEFORE THE EXCAVATIONS.

VIRGINIA.

FRAGMENTS OF A LAY SUNG IN THE FORUM ON THE
DAY WHEREON LUCIUS SEXTIUS SEXTINUS LATE-
RANUS AND CAIUS LICINIUS CALVUS STOLO WERE
ELECTED TRIBUNES OF THE COMMONS THE FIFTH
TIME, IN THE YEAR OF THE CITY CCCLXXXII.

Ye good men of the Commons,
With loving hearts and true,
Who stand by the bold tribunes
That still have stood by you,

Come, make a circle round me,
    And mark my tale with care—
A tale of what Rome once hath borne,
    Of what Rome yet may bear.
This is no Grecian fable,
    Of fountains running wine,   10
Of maids with snaky tresses,
    Or sailors turned to swine.
Here in this very Forum,
    Under the noonday sun,
In sight of all the people,
    The bloody deed was done.
Old men still creep among us
    Who saw that fearful day,
Just seventy years and seven ago,
    When the wicked Ten bare sway.   20

Of all the wicked Ten
    Still the names are held accursed,
And of all the wicked Ten
    Appius Claudius was the worst.
He stalked along the Forum
    Like King Tarquin in his pride ;
Twelve axes waited on him,
    Six marching on a side.
The townsmen shrank to right and left,
    And eyed askance with fear   30
His lowering brow, his curling mouth
    Which alway seemed to sneer.
That brow of hate, that mouth of scorn,
    Marks all the kindred still ;
For never was there Claudius yet
    But wished the Commons ill.
Nor lacks he fit attendance ;
    For close behind his heels,

With outstretched chin and crouching pace,
   The client Marcus steals,   40
His loins girt up to run with speed,
   Be the errand what it may,
And the smile flickering on his cheek
   For aught his lord may say.
Such varlets pimp and jest for hire
   Among the lying Greeks ;
Such varlets still are paid to hoot
   When brave Licinius speaks.
Where'er ye shed the honey,
   The buzzing flies will crowd ;   50
Where'er ye fling the carrion,
   The raven's croak is loud ;
Where'er down Tiber garbage floats,
   The greedy pike ye see ;
And wheresoe'er such lord is found,
   Such client still will be.

Just then, as through one cloudless chink
   In a black stormy sky
Shines out the dewy morning-star,
   A fair young girl came by.   60
With her small tablets in her hand,
   And her satchel on her arm,
Home she went bounding from the school,
   Nor dreamed of shame or harm ;
And past those dreaded axes
   She innocently ran,
With bright, frank brow that had not learned
   To blush at gaze of man ;
And up the Sacred Street she turned,
   And as she danced along   70
She warbled gayly to herself
   Lines of the good old song,

How for a sport the princes
   Came spurring from the camp,
And found Lucrece combing the fleece
   Under the midnight lamp.
The maiden sang as sings the lark
   When up he darts his flight
From his nest in the green April corn
   To meet the morning light;   80
And Appius heard her sweet young voice,
   And saw her sweet young face,
And loved her with the accursed love
   Of his accursed race:
And all along the Forum,
   And up the Sacred Street,
His vulture eye pursued the trip
   Of those small glancing feet.

*   *   *   *   *   *

Over the Alban mountains
   The light of morning broke;   90
From all the roofs of the Seven Hills
   Curled the thin wreaths of smoke:
The city gates were opened;
   The Forum, all alive
With buyers and with sellers,
   Was humming like a hive;
Blithely on brass and timber
   The craftsman's stroke was ringing,
And blithely o'er her panniers
   The market-girl was singing,   100
And blithely young Virginia
   Came smiling from her home—
Ah! woe for young Virginia,
   The sweetest maid in Rome!
With her small tablets in her hand,
   And her satchel on her arm,

Forth she went bounding to the school,
  Nor dreamed of shame or harm.
She crossed the Forum shining
  With stalls in alleys gay,   110
And just had reached the very spot
  Whereon I stand this day,
When up the varlet Marcus came;
  Not such as when erewhile
He crouched behind his patron's heels
  With the true client smile;
He came with lowering forehead,
  Swollen features, and clenched fist,
And strode across Virginia's path,
  And caught her by the wrist.   120
Hard strove the frighted maiden
  And screamed with look aghast,
And at her scream from right and left
  The folk came running fast—
The money-changer Crispus,
  With his thin silver hairs;
And Hanno from the stately booth
  Glittering with Punic wares;
And the strong smith Muræna,
  Grasping a half-forged brand;   130
And Volero the flesher,
  His cleaver in his hand.
All came in wrath and wonder,
  For all knew that fair child,
And as she passed them twice a day
  All kissed their hands and smiled;
And the strong smith Muræna
  Gave Marcus such a blow,
The caitiff reeled three paces back,
  And let the maiden go.   140

Yet glared he fiercely round him,
   And growled in harsh, fell tone,
' She 's mine, and I will have her;
   I seek but for mine own.
She is my slave, born in my house,
   And stolen away and sold,
The year of the sore sickness,
   Ere she was twelve hours old.
'T was in the sad September,
   The month of wail and fright;   150
Two augurs were borne forth that morn,
   The Consul died ere night.
I wait on Appius Claudius,
   I waited on his sire;
Let him who works the client wrong
   Beware the patron's ire!'

So spake the varlet Marcus;
   And dread and silence came
On all the people at the sound
   Of the great Claudian name.   160
For then there was no tribune
   To speak the word of might,
Which makes the rich man tremble,
   And guards the poor man's right.
There was no brave Licinius,
   No honest Sextius then;
But all the city in great fear
   Obeyed the wicked Ten.
Yet ere the varlet Marcus
   Again might seize the maid,   170
Who clung tight to Muræna's skirt
   And sobbed and shrieked for aid,
Forth through the throng of gazers
   The young Icilius pressed,

And stamped his foot, and rent his gown,
  And smote upon his breast,
And sprang upon that column,
  By many a minstrel sung,
Whereon three mouldering helmets,
  Three rusting swords, are hung,   180
And beckoned to the people,
  And in bold voice and clear
Poured thick and fast the burning words
  Which tyrants quake to hear:

'Now, by your children's cradles,
  Now by your fathers' graves,
Be men to-day, Quirites,
  Or be forever slaves!
For this did Servius give us laws!
  For this did Lucrece bleed?   190
For this was the great vengeance wrought
  On Tarquin's evil seed?
For this did those false sons make red
  The axes of their sire?
For this did Scævola's right hand
  Hiss in the Tuscan fire?
Shall the vile fox-earth awe the race
  That stormed the lion's den?
Shall we, who could not brook one lord,
  Crouch to the wicked Ten?   200
O for that ancient spirit
  Which curbed the Senate's will!
O for the tents which in old time
  Whitened the Sacred Hill!
In those brave days our fathers
  Stood firmly side by side;
They faced the Marcian fury,
  They tamed the Fabian pride;

They drove the fiercest Quinctius
  An outcast forth from Rome ;   210
They sent the haughtiest Claudius
  With shivered fasces home.
But what their care bequeathed us
  Our madness flung away ;
All the ripe fruit of threescore years
  Was blighted in a day.
Exult, ye proud patricians !
  The hard-fought fight is o'er.
We strove for honors—'t was in vain ;
  For freedom—'t is no more.   220
No crier to the polling
  Summons the eager throng ;
No tribune breathes the word of might
  That guards the weak from wrong.
Our very hearts, that were so high,
  Sink down beneath your will.
Riches and lands, and power and state—
  Ye have them ; keep them still.
Still keep the holy fillets ;
  Still keep the purple gown,   230
The axes and the curule chair,
  The car and laurel crown ;
Still press us for your cohorts,
  And, when the fight is done,
Still fill your garners from the soil
  Which our good swords have won.
Still, like a spreading ulcer
  Which leech-craft may not cure,
Let your foul usance eat away
  The substance of the poor.   240
Still let your haggard debtors
  Bear all their fathers bore ;

Still let your dens of torment
  Be noisome as of yore—
No fire when Tiber freezes,
  No air in dog-star heat ;
And store of rods for free-born backs,
  And holes for free-born feet.
Heap heavier still the fetters,
  Bar closer still the grate ;   250
Patient as sheep we yield us up
  Unto your cruel hate.
But, by the shades beneath us,
  And by the gods above,
Add not unto your cruel hate
  Your yet more cruel love !
Have ye not graceful ladies,
  Whose spotless lineage springs
From consuls and high pontiffs
  And ancient Alban kings—   260
Ladies who deign not on our paths
  To set their tender feet,
Who from their cars look down with scorn
  Upon the wondering street,
Who in Corinthian mirrors
  Their own proud smiles behold,
And breathe of Capuan odors,
  And shine with Spanish gold ?
Then leave the poor plebeian
  His single tie to life—   270
The sweet, sweet love of daughter,
  Of sister, and of wife ;
The gentle speech, the balm for all
  That his vexed soul endures ;
The kiss, in which he half forgets
  Even such a yoke as yours.

Still let the maiden's beauty swell
   The father's breast with pride ;
Still let the bridegroom's arms infold
   An unpolluted bride.   280
Spare us the inexpiable wrong,
   The unutterable shame,
That turns the coward's heart to steel,
   The sluggard's blood to flame,
Lest, when our latest hope is fled,
   Ye taste of our despair,
And learn by proof in some wild hour
   How much the wretched dare."

*   *   *   *   *   *

Straightway Virginius led the maid
   A little space aside,   290
To where the reeking shambles stood,
   Piled up with horn and hide,
Close to yon low dark archway,
   Where in a crimson flood
Leaps down to the great sewer
   The gurgling stream of blood.
Hard by, a flesher on a block
   Had laid his whittle down ;
Virginius caught the whittle up,
   And hid it in his gown.   300
And then his eyes grew very dim,
   And his throat began to swell,
And in a hoarse, changed voice he spake,
   ' Farewell, sweet child !   Farewell !
O, how I loved my darling !
   Though stern I sometimes be,
To thee, thou know'st, I was not so.
   Who could be so to thee ?
And how my darling loved me !
   How glad she was to hear   310

My footstep on the threshold
    When I came back last year!
And how she danced with pleasure
    To see my civic crown,
And took my sword and hung it up,
    And brought me forth my gown!
Now, all those things are over—
    Yes, all thy pretty ways,
Thy needlework, thy prattle,
    Thy snatches of old lays;   320
And none will grieve when I go forth,
    Or smile when I return,
Or watch beside the old man's bed,
    Or weep upon his urn.
The house that was the happiest
    Within the Roman walls,
The house that envied not the wealth
    Of Capua's marble halls,
Now, for the brightness of thy smile,
    Must have eternal gloom,   330
And for the music of thy voice,
    The silence of the tomb.
The time is come.   See how he points
    His eager hand this way!
See how his eyes gloat on thy grief,
    Like a kite's upon the prey!
With all his wit, he little deems
    That, spurned, betrayed, bereft,
Thy father hath in his despair
    One fearful refuge left.   340
He little deems that in this hand
    I clutch what still can save
Thy gentle youth from taunts and blows,
    The portion of the slave;

Yea, and from nameless evil,
    That passeth taunt and blow—
Foul outrage which thou knowest not,
    Which thou shalt never know.
Then clasp me round the neck once more,
    And give me one more kiss;   350
And now, mine own dear little girl,
    There is no way but this.'
With that he lifted high the steel
    And smote her in the side,
And in her blood she sank to earth,
    And with one sob she died.

Then, for a little moment,
    All people held their breath,
And through the crowded Forum
    Was stillness as of death;   360
And in another moment
    Brake forth from one and all
A cry as if the Volscians
    Were coming o'er the wall.
Some with averted faces
    Shrieking fled home amain;
Some ran to call a leech,
    And some ran to lift the slain;
Some felt her lips and little wrist,
    If life might there be found;   370
And some tore up their garments fast,
    And strove to stanch the wound.
In vain they ran and felt and stanched;
    For never truer blow
That good right arm had dealt in fight
    Against a Volscian foe.

When Appius Claudius saw that deed,
    He shuddered and sank down,

And hid his face some little space
   With the corner of his gown,   380
Till, with white lips and bloodshot eyes,
   Virginius tottered nigh,
And stood before the judgment-seat,
   And held the knife on high:
' O dwellers in the nether gloom,
   Avengers of the slain,
By this dear blood I cry to you,
   Do right between us twain;
And even as Appius Claudius
   Hath dealt by me and mine,   390
Deal you by Appius Claudius
   And all the Claudian line!'
So spake the slayer of his child,
   And turned and went his way;
But first he cast one haggard glance
   To where the body lay,
And writhed, and groaned a fearful groan,
   And then, with steadfast feet,
Strode right across the market-place
   Unto the Sacred Street.   400

Then up sprang Appius Claudius:
   ' Stop him, alive or dead!
Ten thousand pounds of copper
   To the man who brings his head.'
He looked upon his clients,
   But none would work his will;
He looked upon his lictors,
   But they trembled and stood still.
And, as Virginius through the press
   His way in silence cleft,   410
Ever the mighty multitude
   Fell back to right and left.

And he hath passed in safety
   Unto his woful home,
And there ta'en horse to tell the camp
   What deeds are done in Rome.

By this the flood of people
   Was swollen from every side,
And streets and porches round were filled
   With that o'erflowing tide;   420
And close around the body
   Gathered a little train
Of them that were the nearest
   And dearest to the slain.
They brought a bier, and hung it
   With many a cypress crown,
And gently they uplifted her,
   And gently laid her down.
The face of Appius Claudius wore
   The Claudian scowl and sneer,   430
And in the Claudian note he cried,
   'What doth this rabble here?
Have they no crafts to mind at home,
   That hitherward they stray?
Ho! lictors, clear the market-place,
   And fetch the corpse away!'
The voice of grief and fury
   Till then had not been loud;
But a deep sullen murmur
   Wandered among the crowd,   440
Like the moaning noise that goes before
   The whirlwind on the deep,
Or the growl of a fierce watch-dog
   But half-aroused from sleep.
But when the lictors at that word,
   Tall yoemen all and strong,

Each with his axe and sheaf of twigs,
   Went down into the throng,
Those old men say who saw that day
   Of sorrow and of sin   450
That in the Roman Forum
   Was never such a din.
The wailing, hooting, cursing,
   The howls of grief and hate,
Were heard beyond the Pincian Hill,
   Beyond the Latin Gate.
But close around the body,
   Where stood the little train
Of them that were the nearest
   And dearest to the slain,   460
No cries were there, but teeth set fast,
   Low whispers and black frowns,
And breaking-up of benches
   And girding-up of gowns.
'T was well the lictors might not pierce
   To where the maiden lay,
Else surely had they been all twelve
   Torn limb from limb that day.
Right glad they were to struggle back,
   Blood streaming from their heads,   470
With axes all in splinters,
   And raiment all in shreds.
Then Appius Claudius gnawed his lip,
   And the blood left his cheek,
And thrice he beckoned with his hand,
   And thrice he strove to speak;
And thrice the tossing Forum
   Set up a frightful yell:
'See, see, thou dog! what thou hast done,
   And hide thy shame in hell!   480

Thou that wouldst make our maidens slaves
  Must first make slaves of men.
Tribunes! Hurrah for tribunes!
  Down with the wicked Ten!'
And straightway, thick as hailstones,
  Came whizzing through the air
Pebbles and bricks and potsherds
  All round the curule chair;
And upon Appius Claudius
  Great fear and trembling came,   490
For never was a Claudius yet
  Brave against aught but shame.
Though the great houses love us not,
  We own, to do them right,
That the great houses, all save one,
  Have borne them well in fight.
Still Caius of Corioli,
  His triumphs and his wrongs,
His vengeance and his mercy,
  Live in our camp-fire songs.   500
Beneath the yoke of Furius oft
  Have Gaul and Tuscan bowed;
And Rome may bear the pride of him
  Of whom herself is proud.
But evermore a Claudius
  Shrinks from a stricken field,
And changes color like a maid
  At sight of sword and shield.
The Claudian triumphs all were won
  Within the city towers;   510
The Claudian yoke was never pressed
  On any necks but ours.
A Cossus, like a wild-cat,
  Springs ever at the face;

A Fabius rushes like a boar
  Against the shouting chase;
But the vile Claudian litter,
  Raging with currish spite,
Still yelps and snaps at those who run,
  Still runs from those who smite.   520
So now 'twas seen of Appius;
  When stones began to fly,
He shook and crouched, and wrung his hands,
  And smote upon his thigh:
'Kind clients, honest lictors,
  Stand by me in this fray!
Must I be torn in pieces?
  Home, home, the nearest way!'
While yet he spake, and looked around
  With a bewildered stare,   530
Four sturdy lictors put their necks
  Beneath the curule chair;
And fourscore clients on the left,
  And fourscore on the right,
Arrayed themselves with swords and staves,
  And loins girt up for fight.
But, though without or staff or sword,
  So furious was the throng
That scarce the train with might and main
  Could bring their lord along.   540
Twelve times the crowd made at him,
  Five times they seized his gown;
Small chance was his to rise again
  If once they got him down;
And sharper came the pelting,
  And evermore the yell—
'Tribunes! we will have tribunes!'
  Rose with a louder swell.

And the chair tossed as tosses
  A bark with tattered sail   550
When raves the Adriatic
  Beneath an eastern gale,
When the Calabrian sea-marks
  Are lost in clouds of spume,
And the great Thunder-cape has donned
  His veil of inky gloom.
One stone hit Appius in the mouth,
  And one beneath the ear,
And ere he reached Mount Palatine
  He swooned with pain and fear.   560
His cursed head, that he was wont
  To hold so high with pride,
Now, like a drunken man's, hung down
  And swayed from side to side ;
And when his stout retainers
  Had brought him to his door,
His face and neck were all one cake
  Of filth and clotted gore.
As Appius Claudius was that day,
  So may his grandson be !   570
God send Rome one such other sight,
  And send me there to see !

TEMPLE OF VESTA (FROM A COIN).

THE WOLF OF THE CAPITOL.

THE PROPHECY OF CAPYS.

A LAY SUNG AT THE BANQUET IN THE CAPITOL, ON THE DAY WHEREON MANIUS CURIUS DENTATUS, A SECOND TIME CONSUL, TRIUMPHED OVER KING PYRRHUS AND THE TARENTINES, IN THE YEAR OF THE CITY CCCCLXXIX.

I.

Now slain is King Amulius
   Of the great Sylvian line,
Who reigned in Alba Longa
   On the throne of Aventine.
Slain is the Pontiff Camers,
   Who spake the words of doom:
'The children to the Tiber,
   The mother to the tomb.'

II.

In Alba's lake no fisher
  His net to-day is flinging;
On the dark rind of Alba's oaks
  To-day no axe is ringing;
The yoke hangs o'er the manger,
  The scythe lies in the hay;
Through all the Alban villages
  No work is done to-day.

III.

And every Alban burgher
  Hath donned his whitest gown;
And every head in Alba
  Weareth a poplar crown;
And every Alban door-post
  With boughs and flowers is gay;
For to-day the dead are living,
  The lost are found to-day.

IV.

They were doomed by a bloody king,
  They were doomed by a lying priest;
They were cast on the raging flood,
  They were tracked by the raging beast:
Raging beast and raging flood
  Alike have spared the prey;
And to-day the dead are living,
  The lost are found to-day.

V.

The troubled river knew them,
  And smoothed his yellow foam,
And gently rocked the cradle
  That bore the fate of Rome.

The ravening she-wolf knew them,
　　And licked them o'er and o'er,
And gave them of her own fierce milk,
　　Rich with raw flesh and gore.　　　　　40
Twenty winters, twenty springs,
　　Since then have rolled away;
And to-day the dead are living,
　　The lost are found to-day.

VI.

Blithe it was to see the twins,
　　Right goodly youths and tall,
Marching from Alba Longa
　　To their old grandsire's hall.
Along their path fresh garlands
　　Are hung from tree to tree;　　　　　50
Before them stride the pipers,
　　Piping a note of glee.

VII.

On the right goes Romulus,
　　With arms to the elbows red,
And in his hands a broadsword,
　　And on the blade a head—
A head in an iron helmet,
　　With horse-hair hanging down,
A shaggy head, a swarthy head,
　　Fixed in a ghastly frown—　　　　　60
The head of King Amulius
　　Of the great Sylvian line,
Who reigned in Alba Longa
　　On the throne of Aventine.

VIII.

On the left side goes Remus,
　　With wrists and fingers red.

And in his hand a boar-spear,
   And on the point a head—
A wrinkled head and aged,
   With silver beard and hair, 70
And holy fillets round it
   Such as the pontiffs wear—
The head of ancient Camers,
   Who spake the words of doom:
'The children to the Tiber;
   The mother to the tomb.'

IX.

Two and two behind the twins
   Their trusty comrades go,
Four-and-forty valiant men,
   With club and axe and bow. 80
On each side every hamlet
   Pours forth its joyous crowd,
Shouting lads and baying dogs,
   And children laughing loud,
And old men weeping fondly
   As Rhea's boys go by,
And maids who shriek to see the heads,
   Yet, shrieking, press more nigh.

X.

So they marched along the lake;
   They marched by fold and stall, 90
By cornfield and by vineyard,
   Unto the old man's hall.

XI.

In the hall-gate sat Capys,
   Capys the sightless seer;
From head to foot he trembled
   As Romulus drew near.

And up stood stiff his thin white hair,
 And his blind eyes flashed fire:
'Hail! foster-child of the wondrous nurse!
 Hail! son of the wondrous sire! 100

XII.

'But thou—what dost thou here
 In the old man's peaceful hall?
What doth the eagle in the coop,
 The bison in the stall?
Our corn fills many a garner;
 Our vines clasp many a tree;
Our flocks are white on many a hill;
 But these are not for thee.

XIII.

'For thee no treasure ripens
 In the Tartessian mine; 110
For thee no ship brings precious bales
 Across the Libyan brine;
Thou shalt not drink from amber,
 Thou shalt not rest on down;
Arabia shall not steep thy locks,
 Nor Sidon tinge thy gown.

XIV.

'Leave gold and myrrh and jewels,
 Rich table and soft bed,
To them who of man's seed are born,
 Whom woman's milk hath fed. 120
Thou wast not made for lucre,
 For pleasure, nor for rest;
Thou, that art sprung from the War-god's loins,
 And hast tugged at the she-wolf's breast.

XV.

'From sunrise unto sunset
  All earth shall hear thy fame;
A glorious city thou shalt build,
  And name it by thy name:
And there, unquenched through ages,
  Like Vesta's sacred fire,   130
Shall live the spirit of thy nurse,
  The spirit of thy sire.

XVI.

'The ox toils through the furrow,
  Obedient to the goad;
The patient ass up flinty paths
  Plods with his weary load;
With whine and bound the spaniel
  His master's whistle hears;
And the sheep yields her patiently
  To the loud clashing shears.   140

XVII.

'But thy nurse will hear no master,
  Thy nurse will bear no load;
And woe to them that shear her,
  And woe to them that goad!
When all the pack, loud baying,
  Her bloody lair surrounds,
She dies in silence, biting hard,
  Amidst the dying hounds.

XVIII.

'Pomona loves the orchard,
  And Liber loves the vine;   150
And Pales loves the straw-built shed
  Warm with the breath of kine;

And Venus loves the whispers
  Of plighted youth and maid,
In April's ivory moonlight
  Beneath the chestnut shade.

XIX.

'But thy father loves the clashing
  Of broadsword and of shield;
He loves to drink the steam that reeks
  From the fresh battle-field;   160
He smiles a smile more dreadful
  Than his own dreadful frown,
When he sees the thick black cloud of smoke
  Go up from the conquered town.

XX.

'And such as is the War-god,
  The author of thy line,
And such as she who suckled thee,
  Even such be thou and thine!
Leave to the soft Campanian
  His baths and his perfumes;   170
Leave to the sordid race of Tyre
  Their dyeing-vats and looms;
Leave to the sons of Carthage
  The rudder and the oar;
Leave to the Greek his marble nymphs
  And scrolls of wordy lore.

XXI.

'Thine, Roman, is the pilum;
  Roman, the sword is thine,
The even trench, the bristling mound,
  The legion's ordered line;   180

And thine the wheels of triumph
    Which with their laurelled train
Move slowly up the shouting streets
    To Jove's eternal fane.

XXII.

'Beneath thy yoke the Volscian
    Shall vail his lofty brow;
Soft Capua's curled revellers
    Before thy chairs shall bow;
The Lucumoes of Arnus
    Shall quake thy rods to see;   190
And the proud Samnite's heart of steel
    Shall yield to only thee.

XXIII.

'The Gaul shall come against thee
    From the land of snow and night;
Thou shalt give his fair-haired armies
    To the raven and the kite.

XXIV.

'The Greek shall come against thee,
    The conqueror of the East.
Beside him stalks to battle
    The huge earth-shaking beast—   200
The beast on whom the castle
    With all its guards doth stand,
The beast who hath between his eyes
    The serpent for a hand.
First march the bold Epirotes,
    Wedged close with shield and spear,
And the ranks of false Tarentum
    Are glittering in the rear.

XXV.

'The ranks of false Tarentum
  Like hunted sheep shall fly;   210
In vain the bold Epirotes
  Shall round their standards die;
And Apennine's gray vultures
  Shall have a noble feast
On the fat and the eyes
  Of the huge earth-shaking beast.

XXVI.

'Hurrah for the good weapons
  That keep the War-god's land!
Hurrah for Rome's stout pilum
  In a stout Roman hand!   220
Hurrah for Rome's short broadsword
  That through the thick array
Of levelled spears and serried shields
  Hews deep its gory way!

XXVII.

'Hurrah for the great triumph
  That stretches many a mile!
Hurrah for the wan captives
  That pass in endless file!
Ho! bold Epirotes, whither
  Hath the Red King ta'en flight?   230
Ho! dogs of false Tarentum,
  Is not the gown washed white?

XXVIII.

'Hurrah for the great triumph
  That stretches many a mile!
Hurrah for the rich dye of Tyre,
  And the fine web of Nile,

The helmets gay with plumage
   Torn from the pheasant's wings,
The belts set thick with starry gems
   That shone on Indian kings,   240
The urns of massy silver,
   The goblets rough with gold,
The many-colored tablets bright
   With loves and wars of old,
The stone that breathes and struggles,
   The brass that seems to speak!—
Such cunning they who dwell on high
   Have given unto the Greek.

XXIX.

' Hurrah for Manius Curius,
   The bravest son of Rome,   250
Thrice in utmost need sent forth,
   Thrice drawn in triumph home!
Weave, weave, for Manius Curius
   The third embroidered gown;
Make ready the third lofty car,
   And twine the third green crown;
And yoke the steeds of Rosea
   With necks like a bended bow;
And deck the bull, Mevania's bull,
   The bull as white as snow.   260

XXX.

' Blest and thrice blest the Roman
   Who sees Rome's brightest day,
Who sees that long victorious pomp
   Wind down the Sacred Way,
And through the bellowing Forum,
   And round the Suppliants' Grove,
Up to the everlasting gates
   Of Capitolian Jove.

XXXI.

'Then where o'er two bright havens
   The towers of Corinth frown;   270
Where the gigantic King of Day
   On his own Rhodes looks down;
Where soft Orontes murmurs
   Beneath the laurel shades;
Where Nile reflects the endless length
   Of dark-red colonnades;
Where in the still deep water,
   Sheltered from waves and blasts,
Bristles the dusky forest
   Of Byrsa's thousand masts;   280
Where fur-clad hunters wander
   Amidst the Northern ice;
Where through the sand of Morning-land
   The camel bears the spice;
Where Atlas flings his shadow
   Far o'er the western foam,
Shall be great fear on all who hear
   The mighty name of Rome.'

CASTOR AND POLLUX.

NOTES.

ABBREVIATIONS USED IN THE NOTES.

A. S., Anglo-Saxon.
Cf. (*confer*), compare.
Fol., following.
Id. (*idem*), the same.
Skeat, W. W. Skeat's *Concise Etymological Dictionary* (Harper's ed., 1882); or the larger work (Oxford, 1882).

Other abbreviations will be readily understood. The line-numbers in the references to Shakespeare are those of the "Globe" edition, which vary from those of Rolfe's edition only in scenes that are wholly or partly in *prose*.

WALLS OF ROME, FROM THE INSIDE.

NOTES.

HORATIUS.

THE *Lays* were published in 1842, and were popular from the first. Trevelyan (*Life of Macaulay*, Harper's ed. vol. ii. p. 111) says : "Eighteen thousand of the *Lays of Ancient Rome* were sold in ten years ; forty thousand in twenty years ; and by June, 1875, upward of a hundred thousand copies had passed into the hands of readers. But it is a work of superfluity to measure by statistics the success of poems every line of which is, and long has been, too hackneyed for quotation."

Macaulay's introduction to Horatius is as follows:

"There can be little doubt that among those parts of early Roman history which had a poetical origin was the legend of Horatius Cocles. We have several versions of the story, and these versions differ from each other in points of no small importance. Polybius, there is reason to believe, heard the tale recited over the remains of some consul or prætor descended from the old Horatian patricians ; for he introduces it as a specimen of the narratives with which the Romans were in the habit of embellishing their funeral oratory. It is remarkable that, according to him, Horatius defended the bridge alone, and perished in the waters. According to the chronicles which Livy and Dionysius followed, Horatius had two companions, swam safe to shore, and was loaded with honors and rewards.

"These discrepancies are easily explained. Our own literature, indeed, will furnish an exact parallel to what may have taken place at Rome. It is highly probable that the memory of the war of Porsena was preserved by compositions much resembling the two ballads which stand first in the *Reliques of Ancient English Poetry*. In both those ballads the English, commanded by the Percy, fight with the Scots, commanded by the Douglas. In one of the ballads the Douglas is killed by a nameless English archer, and the Percy by a Scottish spearman; in the other, the Percy slays the Douglas in single combat, and is himself made prisoner. In the former, Sir Hugh Montgomery is shot through the heart by a Northumbrian bowman; in the latter he is taken and exchanged for the Percy. Yet both the ballads relate to the same event, and that an event which probably took place within the memory of persons who were alive when both the ballads were made. One of the minstrels says,

> 'Old men that knowen the grounde well yenoughe
> Call it the battell of Otterburn:
> At Otterburn began this spurne
> Upon a monnyn day.
> Ther was the dougghte Doglas slean:
> The Perse never went away.'

The other poet sums up the event in the following lines :

> 'Thys fraye bygan at Otterborne
> Bytwene the nyghte and the day:
> Ther the Dowglas lost hys lyfe,
> And the Percy was lede away.'

"It is by no means unlikely that there were two old Roman lays about the defence of the bridge; and that, while the story which Livy has transmitted to us was preferred by the multitude, the other, which ascribed the whole glory to Horatius alone, may have been the favorite with the Horatian house.

"The following ballad is supposed to have been made about a hundred and twenty years after the war which it celebrates, and just before the taking of Rome by the Gauls. The author seems to have been an honest citizen, proud of the military glory of his country, sick of the disputes of factions, and much given to pining after good old times which had never really existed. The allusion, however, to the partial manner in which the public lands were allotted could proceed only from a plebeian; and the allusion to the fraudulent sale of spoils marks the date of the poem, and shows that the poet shared in the general discontent with which the proceedings of Camillus, after the taking of Veii, were regarded.

"The penultimate syllable of the name *Porsena* has been shortened in spite of the authority of Niebuhr, who pronounces, without assigning any ground for his opinion, that Martial was guilty of a decided blunder in the line,

> 'Hanc spectare manum Porsena non potuit.'

It is not easy to understand how any modern scholar, whatever his attainments may be—and those of Niebuhr were undoubtedly immense—can venture to pronounce that Martial did not know the quantity of a word which he must have uttered and heard uttered a hundred times before he left school. Niebuhr seems also to have forgotten that Martial has fellow-culprits to keep him in countenance. Horace has committed the same decided blunder ; for he gives us, as a pure iambic line,

> ' Minacis aut Etrusca Porsenae manus.'

Silius Italicus has repeatedly offended in the same way, as when he says,

> ' Cernitur effugiens ardentem Porsena dextram ;'

and, again,

> ' Clusinum vulgus, cum, Porsena magne, jubebas.'

A modern writer may be content to err in such company.

"Niebuhr's supposition that each of the three defenders of the bridge was the representative of one of the three patrician tribes is both ingenious and probable, and has been adopted in the following poem."

1. *Lars Porsena. Lars, Lar,* or *Larth* was a title of honor given to nearly all the Etruscan kings. Another example of it is *Lar Tolumnius,* King of Veii, whom Cossus slew in single combat (see on 190 below). It is the same word as the English *Lord.* Cf. Tennyson, *Princess,* ii. 113 : "That lay at wine with Lar and Lucumo."

Porsĕna is also written *Porsenna* and *Porsina.* As Macaulay remarks, the form with the short *e* occurs in Martial (i. 22. 6), Horace (*Epodes,* 16. 4), and Silius (viii. 391, 480 ; x. 484, 502). *Porsenna* occurs in Virgil (*Æneid,* viii. 646), etc. The Greek writers always make the penult long.

Porsena was king of the Etruscan town of Clusium, where, according to the legend, Tarquinius Superbus applied for help, after seeking it in vain from Veii and Tarquinii. Porsena, as Tacitus tells us (*Hist.* iii. 72), completely conquered Rome. The tale of his repulse by Horatius and his two companions was an invention of Roman vanity, to conceal the great disaster of their city. This expedition of Porsena was kept in the minds of the Romans of later times by the custom at auctions of offering for sale first "the goods of King Porsena." As Niebuhr thinks, this may have arisen from the circumstance that, when the Romans threw off the Tuscan yoke, they obtained possession of property within the city belonging to Porsena, which they sold at auction.

Clusium became prominent in the time of Porsena from the personal abilities of that monarch, who is represented by Livy simply as ruler of Clusium, and is called King of the Etruscans only by later rhetorical writers. It was an inland city of Etruria, in the valley of the Clanis (cf. 38 below), and was one of the twelve cities of the Etruscan confederation. In the time of Tarquinius Priscus, when she gave Rome a dynasty, Etruria possessed the land of the Volscians and the whole of Campania. This great extent of territory was divided into Etruria proper, Etruria Circumpadana, and Etruria Campaniana. Each of these districts was divided into twelve states, each represented by a city. No list of the twelve cities of Etruria proper has been given by ancient writers. They were probably Tarquinii, Veii, Falerii, Cære, Volsinii, Vetulonia, Rasellæ, Clusium, Arretium, Cortona, Perusia, and Volaterræ. *Chiusi*, the modern Clusium, shows few traces of her ancient greatness, but is rich in Etruscan relics. The celebrated tomb of Porsena, a description of which from Varro is given by Pliny, is by some believed to have been discovered near Chiusi, but there is little or no ground for the belief, and the account itself is probably fabulous.

2. *The Nine Gods.* Pliny (*Nat. Hist.* ii. 53) tells us that the Etruscans believed in Nine Great Gods, who alone had the power of hurling thunderbolts—the *Dei Novensiles.* **The term really means the** *new* **(not native) gods, from** *novus-insideo.*

6. *A trysting-day.* A day of meeting. A *tryst* is properly a pledge. It is the same word as *trust.*

14. *Etruscan.* The name *Etruria* is almost universally used by classical Latin writers. The term *Tuscia*, preserved in the modern *Tuscany,* occurs often in later times, and was the official designation of the province in the time of the Empire. The people, on the other hand, were at all times called indifferently *Etrusci* or *Tusci,* the latter being apparently the more ancient form. The Greeks called them *Tyrrhenians,* while the native name of the people was *Rasena* or *Rasenna.* The Etruscans were of a different race from the Romans, and spoke a radically different language. The origin of the race is very uncertain. Mommsen, in his *History of Rome,* says : " 'The Etruscans,' Dionysius said long ago, ' are like no other nation in language and manners ;' and we have nothing to add to this statement."

19. *Amain.* With full power. The prefix, which occurs in such words as *abed, afoot, asleep,* and the like, is the A. S. *on, an,* or *a,* signifying *in* or *with.*

22. *Hamlet.* The word is a diminutive from A. S. *ham,* English *home.*

24. *Like an eagle's nest.* Cf. Horace, *Odes,* iii. 4. 14 : "celsae nidum Acherontiae" (of a town nestling on the edge of a hill). The commanding situation of the village is well described by *hangs.* For a similar expression cf. Virgil, *Eclogues,* i. 75 :

> "Non ego vos posthac, viridi proiectus in antro,
> Dumosa pendere procul de rupe videbo."

26. *Volaterræ.* The Etruscan *Velathri,* one of the most ancient and powerful cities of Etruria, five miles north of the Cecina river and fifteen from the sea. It had an extremely commanding situation 1700 feet above the sea, on the summit of a hill bounded on all sides by precipices. It was the last stronghold of the Marian party in Italy, and yielded only after a two years' siege conducted by Sulla in person. The modern town (*Volterra*) retains large portions of the ancient walls, 40 feet high and 13 feet thick, and one of the gateways (*Porta dell' Arco*), 20 feet high.

27. *Hold.* Stronghold, fortress ; as in Shakespeare, 2 *Hen. IV.* ind. 35 : "this worm-eaten hold of ragged stone " (the castle of the Earl of Northumberland), etc. Cf. *keep* as applied to the central tower of a castle.

30. *Populonia.* The principal maritime city of Etruria, originally called *Pupluna.* Strabo says it was the only one of the ancient Etruscan cities

ANCIENT GATEWAY, VOLATERRÆ.

which was situated on the sea-coast. It became prosperous from its connection with the neighboring island of Ilva (see on 303 below), the iron
from whose mines was carried to Populonia to be smelted and thence
exported. In 205 B.C., when Scipio was fitting out his fleet to go to
Africa, Populonia undertook to supply him with iron. Servius (on
Æneid, x. 172) states that the town was founded by Corsicans, and that
it was of later date than the Etruscan league. Like many of the Etruscan cities, it was built upon a lofty hill. At the highest point of the hill
stood a lonely watch-tower, from which Strabo says that both Corsica and
Sardinia were visible. The latter part of the statement, though repeated
by many writers, is erroneous, for even if the distance were not too great,
the nearer mountains of Elba would shut out those of Sardinia from the
view. Populonia was the only city of Etruria which had a silver coinage
of its own. It was of a peculiar character; the reverse was generally
plain, not *incuse*, or indented, like most of the ancient Greek coins, while
the obverse bore a Gorgon's head. Populonia sustained a siege by Sulla
at the same time as Volaterræ, and never recovered from the blow which
it received. In the Middle Ages a feudal castle was erected on the site,
which, with a few adjacent houses, still bears the name of Populonia, and
is a conspicuous object from a distance.

34. *Mart.* A contracted form of *market ;* from the Latin *mercatus*
Cf. *Hamlet*, i. 1. 74: " And foreign mart for implements of war."

Pisæ. An important city of Etruria on the northern bank of the Arnus, a few miles from its mouth. Very little is known of its early history. The identity of its name with that of the city in Elis naturally led to the supposition that one was derived from the other (Virgil, *Æneid*, x. 179), but Cato considered it of genuine Etruscan origin. In Pliny's time it had become a thriving town, and during the Middle Ages it was one of the most flourishing commercial cities in Italy. It was on the site of the modern Pisa, though great natural changes have taken place in the locality.

36. *Massilia.* The modern Marseilles. It was founded by the Phocæans (from the Ionian town of Phocæa in Asia). It was a rich and prosperous city, with an extensive commerce. Like all the Greeks, the Massilians had slaves, readily obtained from the *fair-haired* Gauls, who sold their own children for this purpose. Cf. *Capys*, 195.

Triremes. Ships with three banks of oars, as the name implies. Up to the time of the first Punic war these were the largest vessels in the Roman navy, but later *quadriremes, quinqueremes*, etc., were built.

38. *Clanis.* A river in the territory of Clusium, flowing into the Tiber. It drains a remarkable valley, thirty miles long, and so level that the waters from the surrounding hills would flow almost indifferently in either direction. We learn from Tacitus that as early as A.D. 15 a project was formed of turning aside the waters of the Clanis (or the *Chiana,** as it is now called) into the Arnus; but the plan was not carried out until the last century. The valley had become marshy and malarious from frequent inundations, but is now well-drained, healthy, and very fertile.

40. *Cortona.* A very ancient city of Etruria, between Arretium and Clusium, on a lofty hill about nine miles from Lake Trasimenus. It was one of the most powerful cities of the Confederation. We hear very little about it in later times, for its almost impregnable situation rendered it free from attack. The modern city of Cortona is the see of a bishop, and has a population of about 5000. Its walls are for the most part based on the ancient walls, and it is rich in Etruscan remains.

43. *Auser.* A river of Etruria, rising on the borders of Liguria, and flowing into the Arnus. The modern river, the *Serchio* (supposed to be a corruption of *Auserculus*), flows into the Tyrrhenian Sea seven miles north of the mouth of the Arno. The whole space between the two rivers in the lower part of their course is so flat and low that their waters still communicate during great floods.

Rill is cognate with the Latin *rima* (see Virgil, *Æneid*, i. 123: "rimisque fatiscunt"), and strictly means a shallow trench or channel.

44. *Champ.* To eat noisily; cognate with *chew, jaw*, and the Greek γαμφαί (jaws).

45. *The Ciminian hill.* Mt. Ciminus (*Monte Cimino*), the culminating point of a range of volcanic heights, extending from near the Tiber in a southwesterly direction towards the sea. It is a conspicuous object from Rome, and separates the *Campagna* from the plains of Central Etruria.

---

* In the Italian the lost Latin *l* is replaced by *i*; as in *Chiusi* (*Clusium*), *Firenze* (*Florentia*), *piombo* (*plumbum*), etc.

It was covered in ancient times (as part of it still is) with a dense forest, called *Silva Ciminia*, which was regarded by the early Romans with no less awe than the Hercynian Forest was in later times. It abounded in game.

46. *Clitumnus.* A small river in Umbria, celebrated for the clearness of its waters, and for the beauty of the cattle which pastured on its banks. These cattle, of a pure white color (cf. 55 below) and large size, were set apart as victims to be slaughtered at triumphs or other special ceremonies (see on *Capys*, 259 below). Their color was thought to be due to their drinking and bathing in the extremely pure waters of the Clitumnus; but, though the same tradition is preserved to-day, the cattle are no longer remarkable for their whiteness. Pliny describes the source of the river in such a way as to show that it was considered a sight worth visiting. Caligula undertook a journey for that express purpose, and Honorius turned aside from his progress along the Flaminian Way for the same object. Cf. Byron, *Childe Harold*, iv. 67 :

> "But thou, Clitumnus, in thy sweetest wave
> Of the most living crystal that was e'er
> The haunt of river nymph, to gaze and lave
> Her limbs where nothing hid them, thou dost rear
> Thy grassy banks whereon the milk-white steer
> Grazes; the purest god of gentle waters,
> And most serene of aspect and most clear!
> Surely that stream was unprofaned by slaughters—
> A mirror and a bath for Beauty's youngest daughters!"

49. *Volsinian mere.* A lake of southern Etruria nearly as large as Lake Trasimenus. It took its name from the town of Volsinii, on its northeastern shore. It is sometimes called the *Tarquinian Lake*, because its western shore adjoined the territory of Tarquinii. The word *mere* (Latin *mare*) is cognate with *mortal*, and strictly means a dead or desert waste of water.

58. *Arretium.* One of the most ancient and powerful cities of Etruria, situated in the upper valley of the Arnus, about four miles south of the river. It was undoubtedly one of the twelve cities of the League, and also one of the five which aided the Latins against Tarquinius Priscus. After the Romans had conquered Italy, it became an important military post, commanding as it did the western entrance into Etruria and the valley of the Tiber from Cisalpine Gaul. Mæcenas, the friend and counsellor of Augustus, is said to have been a native of Arretium, and, while there is no proof that he himself was born there, the family of the Cilnii, to which he belonged, was at an early period the most powerful and conspicuous of the nobility of that city. See Horace, *Odes*, iii. 29. 1 : "Tyrrhena regum progenies;" *Satires*, i. 6. 1 (where there is an allusion to the supposed Lydian origin of the Etruscans):

> "Non quia, Maecenas, Lydorum quicquid Etruscos
> Incolunt fines, nemo generosior est te."

In more recent times the city (the modern *Arezzo*) was noted as the birthplace of Petrarch. Many of the most interesting specimens of Etruscan art have been discovered here, including much pottery, of a peculiar style of bright red ware with ornaments in relief, wholly different from the painted vases so common in southern Etruria. Roman inscriptions on the articles confirm the statement of Pliny, who speaks of Arretium as still celebrated in his time for its pottery; which was, however, regarded with contempt by the wealthy Romans, and used only for humble purposes.

59. *Old men.* Too old for military service, as the *young boys* were too young. In Rome every citizen more than seventeen and less than forty-six years old was obliged to serve in the army when required.

60. *Umbro.* A river of Etruria, next in size to the Arnus, flowing into the sea about sixteen miles north of the promontory of *Mons Argentarius*. The name is supposed to be connected with the Umbrians, who held that part of Italy before its conquest by the Etruscans; and Pliny tells us that the coast district as far south as Telamon was called "Tractus Umbriae."

62. *Luna.* A city of Etruria on the left bank of the Macra near its mouth, and hence on the very borders of Liguria. Indeed, it had fallen into the hands of the Ligurians before that people came in contact with the Romans. There is no ground for considering it a city of the League. Luna was noted for its wine, which was considered the best in Etruria; for its cheeses, some of which weighed a thousand pounds; and for its marble (similar to that of the modern Carrara, only a few miles from the ruins of Luna), which was equal to the best Parian. The buildings of Luna and even its walls are said to have been built of this stone, whence Rutilius calls them "candentia moenia." The city fell to decay under the Roman emperors, and was finally destroyed by the Arabs in 1016.

63. *Must.* New wine, or *mustum*; whence *moist*, *musty*, and *mustard* (this last because it was mixed with must or vinegar).

68. *Alway.* Originally two words, *all* and *way* (= all the way, probably at first in reference to space traversed, but at a very early period transferred to time); afterwards confused with the genitive *always*, which has superseded it in prose, *alway* being now archaic and poetic. Cf. *Matt.* xxviii. 20, etc.

71. *Verses.* Predictions, prophecies. Compare the use (mostly poetical) of *carmina*; as in *Æneid*, vi. 74, etc.

72. *Traced from the right.* The Etruscans retained down to the latest period the mode of writing from right to left. Lucretius says (vi. 381): "Tyrrhena retro volventem carmina frustra."

73. *Yore.* Originally the genitive plural of the A. S. word for *year*, so that the sense was *of years*, that is, in years past.

80. *Nurscia*, or *Nortia*, was the Etruscan goddess of fortune, apparently identical with *Fortuna* of Antium and Præneste. She was worshipped at Volsinii, where a nail was driven every year into the wall of her temple for the purpose of marking the number of years.

81. *The golden shields of Rome.* The twelve sacred shields (*ancilia*) preserved in the temple of Mars Gradivus on the Palatine Hill. According to one legend, a shield was found in the palace of Numa which was supposed to have fallen from heaven, as it could not be learned that any human hand had brought it there. The haruspices declared that the

Roman state would endure so long as this shield was kept in Rome. To secure its preservation, Numa had eleven other shields made exactly like it; and twelve priests, known as the *Salii,* were appointed to take care of the twelve shields. At the yearly feast of the god, on the calends of March, the Salii carried the *ancilia* about the city, at the same time singing sacred songs and performing a kind of dance, in which they kept time by striking the shields with rods. The cut shows one of these rods, and also the Salii on their march. The material of the shields is not mentioned by ancient writers, but, according to the later grammarians, it was bronze, not gold.

ANCILIA CARRIED BY SALII.

83. *Tale.* A number, reckoning; like *tally* from *tell* (=count).

86. *Sutrium.* A small town in the southern part of Etruria, about thirty-two miles from Rome. It never became a place of any importance, but its position on the Cassian Way preserved it from falling into decay, like so many of the Etruscan cities, under the Roman Empire. The modern town, *Sutri,* has only 2000 inhabitants, but retains the episcopal see which it held throughout the Middle Ages. It contains a remarkable amphitheatre, excavated in the tufa rock.

95. *Muster.* A fair show, an assembly (from Latin *monstro*).

96. *Tusculan Mamilius.* The *Mamilia gens* was one of the most distinguished families of Tusculum, and indeed in the whole of Latium. They traced their origin to the mythical Mamilia, daughter of Telegonus, the son of Odysseus and Circe. Their coins bear on one side a head of Mercury, and on the other Odysseus in his travelling dress with his dog. Mamilius was the foremost man of the Latin race in the time of Tarquinius Superbus, who secured his alliance by giving him his daughter in marriage.

Tusculum was a strong city of Latium fifteen miles from Rome. It was said to have been founded by Telegonus. After the final defeat of Tarquin at Lake Regillus, Tusculum remained for a long time a faithful ally of Rome. In the great Latin war it opposed Rome, but after the defeat of the Latins the Tusculans were treated with great indulgence. In later times Tusculum was one of the favorite resorts of the wealthy Romans. Here Lucullus, Cato, Cicero, and others had villas, and Cicero composed many of his philosophical works. The ancient city remained entire until nearly the end of the twelfth century, and its ruins are still to be seen near the modern Frascati.

98. *The yellow Tiber. Flavus* (yellow) is a constant epithet applied to the Tiber by Roman poets. Cf. 466 and 470 below, and Horace, *Odes,* i. 2. 13 :

"Vidimus flavum Tiberim retortis
Litore Etrusco violenter undis
Ire deiectum monumenta regis
Templaque Vestae," etc.

100. *Champaign.* Open country, plains. See Shakespeare, *Lear*, i. 1. 57 : "With shadowy forests and with champaigns rich'd ;" also *Twelfth Night*, ii. 5. 174 : "Daylight and champaign discovers not more." In *Lucrece* (1247) the word is used as an adjective : "A goodly champaign plain."

106. *Folk.* Properly a collective noun (=a crowd of people), though it has come to be used in the plural. It is allied to *flock*.

110. *Litters* (*lecticæ*) for sick persons and invalids seem to have been in use at Rome (as in Greece) from the earliest times. They were covered, and enclosed with curtains or with sides in which there were windows. In later times they were used by people in health, especially in travelling. They were carried by means of poles attached but not fixed to the litter. The poles rested on the shoulders of the bearers, and not on thongs passed around their necks, as some modern writers have thought. In the time of the Empire their use in the city became general. They were carried by tall, handsome slaves in gorgeous liveries.

115. *Skins of wine.* When wine was transported from one place to another, it was put into bags of goat-skin, well pitched over, so as to make the seams perfectly tight. When the quantity was large, a number of hides were sewed together, and the leather tun thus made was carried in a cart.

117. *Kine.* The old plural of *cow.* It is really a double plural (like *brethren*), the A. S. *cú* having

SILENUS ASTRIDE UPON A WINE-SKIN.

the plural *cý,* whence the Middle English *ky,* which was pluralized by adding *en* (as in *oxen*), forming *ky-en,* or *kine.*

122. *The rock Tarpeian.* A steep rock on the Saturnian Hill (from an early period called the Capitoline), from which traitors were hurled. Tarpeia, according to the legend, was a Roman maiden, who treacherously opened the citadel to the Sabines. She stipulated that her reward should be "what they wore on their left arms," meaning their golden bracelets, but they cast upon her their shields, which they bore on their left arms, and crushed her. Cf. Byron, *Childe Harold*, iv. 112 :

" Where is the rock of Triumph, the high place
  Where Rome embraced her heroes? where the steep
  Tarpeian—fittest goal of Treason's race,
  The promontory whence the Traitor's Leap
  Cured all ambition?"

In the present passage *the rock Tarpeian* is probably used for the hill in general. The precise location of the part from which traitors were thrown is now matter of dispute, but the weight of authority seems to be in favor of the south side, or the *Monte Caprino*, as it is called.

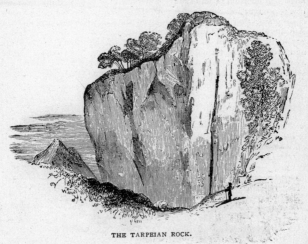

THE TARPEIAN ROCK.

123. *Wan.* The original sense of the word seems to have been tired out, from which the transition is easy to pale from fatigue.

Burghers. Citizens. The word is cognate with *burgess*, which in Mommsen's *History of Rome* (English translation) is the designation of the Roman citizens. It is derived from *borough+er*.

126. *The Fathers of the City.* The *Patres Conscripti*, or senators. See on *Lake Regillus*, 119 below.

133. *Crustumerium.* An ancient city of Latium, on the borders of the Sabine territory, between Fidenæ and Eretum. It was reckoned by Plutarch as a Sabine city, but Virgil (*Æneid*, vii. 631) mentions it among the five great cities which were the first to take up arms against Æneas, all which he undoubtedly regarded as Latin towns. The country about Crustumerium was noted for its fertility. It produced great quantities of corn, and Virgil (*Georgics*, ii. 88) says that pears were produced there in great abundance which were red only on one side, a peculiarity which they still retain.

9

134. *Verbenna.* This name is one of Macaulay's own invention; it is not mentioned by any Roman writer.

Ostia. The seaport of Rome, at the mouth of the Tiber, sixteen miles from the city. All ancient writers agree that it was founded by Ancus Martius, who at the same time established salt-works there, which for a long time supplied Rome and the neighboring country. Ostia was always a colony of Rome and never became independent. Although it must have grown in importance with the increasing power of Rome, no historical mention is made of the town until the second Punic War, when it was a naval and commercial port of the highest importance. From its close connection with Rome it enjoyed special privileges, and Ostia and Antium alone were granted exemption from levies for military service in 207 B.C. It suffered during the wars of Marius and Sulla, and was taken and sacked by the former in 87 B.C. In 67 B.C. a fleet which had been assembled there to suppress the pirates was attacked by the pirates themselves and destroyed (Cicero, *Pro Leg. Manil.* 12. 33).

OSTIA.

The modern village of Ostia is an insignificant place, the climate of which in summer is extremely unhealthy. It has scarcely a hundred inhabitants, most of whom are employed in the salt-works. The site of the ancient town is now three miles from the mouth of the river. In the time of Strabo the port had been seriously injured by alluvial deposits, and among the projects of Julius Cæsar was one for its improvement. Claudius carried out the plan by constructing an entirely new harbor two miles to the north; but this being also filled up, Trajan in A.D. 103 began a new one at the modern *Porto*, which was choked in its turn. The castle, which is now the most conspicuous object at Ostia, was built in the early part of the 16th century.

136. *Astur.* Another name of Macaulay's invention. There is a Latin word *astur* meaning a hawk.

Janiculum. A hill across the Tiber opposite the Campus Martius, where the river bends farthest to the west. In the time of Tarquin it did not form part of the city, but it had been fortified by Ancus Martius as an outpost and connected with the city by the *Pons Sublicius.* It is said to have been called *Janiculum* from Janus, a deified king of Latium, who had a citadel there.

138. *I wis.* Not a verb and pronoun, although often so considered, and apparently so regarded by Shakespeare and his contemporaries. It is an adverb meaning certainly, and was at first written *ywis.* Cf. the German *gewiss.*

The Senate. The Latin word *senatus* means a collection of old men. See Cicero, *De Senectute,* vi. 19 : " Quae [consilium, ratio, sententia] nisi essent in senibus, non summum consilium nostri maiores appellassent senatum ;" and compare the Greek (Lacedæmonian) γερουσία. The Roman senate at this time consisted of 300 members, 100 from each of the three tribes, and this remained the regular number for many centuries. The senators held their office for life, unless expelled by the censors for unbecoming conduct. They were chosen, at first by the consul but afterwards by the censors, from those who had held high offices in the state. After the time of Sulla, every man who had held the quæstorship, or any higher office, might sit in the senate, so that the number sometimes reached five or six hundred.

The original purpose of the senate was to give advice to the kings, and its decrees were at all times called *consulta,* that is, matters which seemed advisable. At an early period, however, the senate, though it did not have authority to pass laws and was itself subject to the laws, became the ruling power in the state, and by its *consulta* controlled the whole Roman world. The senate met regularly three times a month, and could be specially summoned by the consul, or (in later times) by a tribune of the people, and the magistrate who summoned it presided at its meetings. In the later days of the Republic, the members of the senate formed an *order* (see on *Lake Regillus,* 3 below), called the *ordo senatorius,* an hereditary nobility. The members of the order wore a tunic with a broad purple stripe and a shoe of a peculiar pattern ; they also sat in the orchestra at the theatres and amphitheatres.

142. *The Consul.* After the expulsion of the kings, the chief magistracy of the state was represented by two officers, elected annually, called at first *prætors,* or leaders, but very soon afterwards *consuls,* a word of uncertain origin, but probably derived from *con*+the root of *salio* (cf. *exsul, praesul*), meaning perhaps those who go together. In the early days of the Republic the power of the consuls was nearly equal to that of the kings who had preceded them, but with the establishment of the prætorship, censorship, etc., their power was diminished. Until 366 B.C. the consulship was open only to patricians, but it finally became a principle of the Roman constitution that both consuls should not be patricians. The consuls presided in the senate, and in the comitia of the centuries, and were preceded by twelve lictors (see on *Lake Regillus,* 2 below), enjoying these honors for a month at a time in turn. In time of war they commanded the army, and a consul might be given dictatorial power by the senate (see on *Lake Regillus,* 123). After the Roman rule had ex-

ROMAN CONSUL.

tended beyond the boundaries of Italy, the consuls governed a province as *proconsuls* at the close of their term of office.

144. *They girded up their gowns.* The cumbrous form of the toga, which was always worn in the senate, made it necessary to gird it up whenever active work was to be done. Cf. Virgil, *Æneid,* i. 210: "Illi se praedae accingunt ;" and *Id.* ii. 235: "Accingunt omnes operi."

147. *The River-Gate.* The *Porta Flumentana* must have been in the short piece of wall between the Capitoline Hill and the Tiber. Its situation near the river may be inferred from its name, from the fact that Livy mentions it in connection with inundations, and from a passage in Varro (*R. R.* iii. 2).

150. *Roundly.* Plainly, "without circumlocution" (as the dictionaries define it, though at first it seems very like a bull). Cf. Shakespeare, *As You Like It*, v. 3. 11 : "Shall we clap into 't roundly, without hawking or spitting or saying we are hoarse ?" So the adjective *round* = blunt, unceremonious ; as in *Twelfth Night*, ii. 3. 102 : "I must be round with you," etc.

151. *The bridge.* The *Pons Sublicius,* the oldest and most frequently mentioned of the Roman bridges, was a wooden bridge said to have been built by Ancus Martius. It connected the Janiculum with the city, but its exact site is a vexed question. It was of great religious importance, and was under the special protection of one of the *pontifices.* Even after a new bridge of stone was built beside it for purposes of traffic, the wooden bridge was kept in repair as a venerable and sacred relic, and as indispensable in certain religious ceremonies (see on *Lake Regillus,* 697 below). It is known to have been in existence in the time of Constantine. Pliny (*Nat. Hist.* xxxvi. 23) tells us that, on account of the difficulty and delay in breaking it down on this occasion, it was reconstructed without nails, in such a manner that each beam could be removed and replaced at pleasure.

156. *Sir Consul.* When the poem was first published certain critics made fun of this, and suggested " O Consul " in place of it; but the expression is in keeping with the old ballad style which Macaulay imitates, and it is mere pedantry to object to it. Shakespeare has *Sir* repeatedly in the Roman plays ; as in *Julius Cæsar,* iv. 3. 246, 250, *Coriolanus,* i. 5. 15, iv. 5. 142. Cf. *Acts,* vii. 26, xiv. 15, xvi. 30, etc. *Sir* is of Latin origin (from *senior,* through the French).

160–173. *And saw the swarthy storm of dust,* etc. For a prose description of a similar scene, vivid from its very simplicity, cf. Xenophon, *Anabasis,* i. 8. 8.

177. *Twelve fair cities.* The twelve cities of the Etruscan Confederation. See on 1 above.

180. *The Umbrian.* Umbria is the northeastern division of Italy proper, east of Etruria. The Etruscans engaged in many wars with the Umbrians and with their neighbors the Gauls. The former at one time possessed a great part of Etruria, from which they were driven at a very early period after a long struggle, with the loss of three hundred towns. The Umbrians are regarded by all writers of antiquity as the most ancient people of Italy.

184. *By port and vest.* By bearing and dress. *Port* is from the Latin *portare, vest* from *vestis.* For a similar use of the latter word see Fuller, *Worthies :* " He much affected to appear in foreign vests," etc.

Crest. The plume or tuft on the top of the helmet, by which the wearer was most readily distinguished in a throng of warriors. Cf. Tennyson, *Oriana :* " She watched my crest among them all," etc.

185. *Lucumo.* Literally, one possessed or inspired ; a title given to Etruscan priests and princes, like the Roman *patricius.* It was mistaken by the Romans for a proper name. The title was given to the son of Demaratus, King of Corinth, afterwards Tarquinius Priscus. See on 1 above.

186. *Cilnius.* The *Cilnii* were a powerful Etruscan family, who seem to have been unusually firm supporters of the Roman interests. They were *lucumones* in their city, Arretium. The name has been rendered famous by C. Cilnius Mæcenas, the intimate friend of Augustus. See on 58 above.

188. *Fourfold shield.* Made of four thicknesses of hide. Such shields

were made of wood or wicker, which was covered with ox-hides of several folds, and finally bound around the edge with metal. See Homer, *Iliad*, xii. 294 fol. :

> αὐτίκα δ᾽ ἀσπίδα μὲν προσθ᾽ ἔσχετο πάντοσ᾽ ἐΐσην,
> καλὴν χαλκείην ἐξήλατον, ἣν ἄρα χαλκεὺς
> ἤλασεν, ἔντοσθεν δὲ βοείας ῥάψε θαμειὰς
> χρυσείῃς ῥάβδοισι διηνεκέσιν περὶ κύκλον.

The arms of the Etruscans closely resembled those of the Greeks.

189. *Brand*. A sword, from its brightness. The succession of meanings is (1) a burning ; (2) a firebrand ; (3) a sword-blade.

190. *Tolumnius*. Probably king of Veii. In 438 B.C. a king of Veii of the same name was slain in single combat by Cornelius Cossus, who, following the example of Romulus, consecrated the spoils to Jupiter Feretrius ; the second case in which the *spolia opima* were won.

192. *Thrasymene*. The most approved spellings in the Latin are *Trasumenus* and *Trasymenus*. There is no authority for the *Th*. It is the largest lake in Etruria, situated in the eastern part between Cortona and Perusia (Perugia), from the latter of which it is now sometimes called *Lago di Perugia*. It is about thirty miles in circumference, but of

LAKE THRASYMENE.

small depth, nowhere exceeding thirty feet, and its banks are low, flat, and covered with reeds. It is famous for the crushing defeat of the Roman consul C. Flamininus by Hannibal (217 B.C.) in "the defiles fatal to Roman rashness." Livy relates a story that the fury of the combatants was such that they were unconscious of an earthquake shock which occurred during the battle. See Byron, *Childe Harold*, iv. 73 :

"And such the shock of battle on this day
And such the frenzy, whose convulsion blinds
To all save carnage, that, beneath the fray,
An earthquake rolled unheedingly away."

193. *Fast by.* Fixed, or made fast, by ; like *hard* (firm) *by* and *close by*. Cf. *Winter's Tale*, iv. 4. 512 : " A vessel rides fast by," etc.

196. *His ivory car.* The ancients used ivory on a more extensive scale than is known in modern times. The statue of the Olympian Zeus by Phidias was made of it or covered with it. The Romans, who obtained large quantities from Africa, also used it in works of art and ornament of considerable size.

199. *False Sextus.* Sextus Tarquinius, the second son of Tarquinius Superbus.

200. *The deed of shame.* The rape of Lucrece, the immediate cause of the expulsion of Tarquin. See Shakespeare, *Lucrece*, and Ovid, *Fasti*, book ii.

The first reading of this line was " That brought Lucrece to shame." Macaulay altered it here and elsewhere at the suggestion of his friend, Mr. Thomas Flower Ellis. See Trevelyan's *Life* (Harper's ed. vol. ii. p. 108).

217. *Horatius.* The Horatian gens was a patrician family belonging to the tribe of Luceres. The burghers or patricians consisted originally of three distinct tribes : the *Ramnes*, a Latin colony on the Palatine hill, said to have been founded by Romulus ; the *Tities*, or Sabine settlers on the Quirinal and Viminal hills, under King Tatius ; and the *Luceres*, mostly Etruscans, who had settled on the Cælian. As mentioned in the introduction, the three defenders of the bridge were representatives of these three tribes. Horatius bore the surname *Cocles*, or "the one-eyed."

218. *The Captain of the Gate.* Apparently not a permanent office, but an appointment for this special occasion. Livy (ii. 10) says : " qui positus forte in statione pontis," etc.

229. *The holy maidens.* The virgin priestesses of Vesta, six in number, two from each of the original three tribes. It was their chief duty to watch by turns, night and day, the " eternal flame " on the altar of Vesta, the extinction of which was considered to portend the destruction of the state. They were held in high honor and were granted certain immunities and privileges.

237. *Strait.* Narrow (Latin *strictus*); misprinted " straight " in some editions.

241. *Spurius Lartius.* The *Lartia gens* was a patrician family of Etruscan origin. The name is probably derived from *Lar*. The family disappears early from history, the only other famous member being T. Lartius, the first dictator, in 501 B.C. See on *Lake Regillus*, 123 below.

242. *A Ramnian.* See on 217 above.

245. *Herminius.* The *Herminia gens* was a very ancient patrician family at Rome, which also vanishes early from history. The syllable *Her* is common in Sabellian names, but one of the family bore the præ-nomen *Lar*, *Larius*, or *Larcius*, which is undoubtedly of Etruscan origin,

and the Roman antiquaries regarded the family as Etruscan. It is remarkable that Herminius and Lartius are coupled in their first consulship, at the bridge, and in the battle of Lake Regillus.

246. *A Titian.* See on 217 above.

261. *Then lands were fairly portioned.* A standing grievance of the
plebeians was that the *ager publicus* (see on 542 below), or land which was
the property of the state, acquired by conquest, was occupied almost entirely by the patricians, until the passing of the Licinian laws.

262. *Then spoils were fairly sold.* As stated in the introduction, this
line places the date of the composition of this poem after the capture of
Veii in 396 B.C. An immense amount of booty was taken at Veii, which
was distributed among the citizens. In 391 B.C. Camillus, who had commanded the Romans at Veii, was accused by L. Appuleius, tribune of the
people, of having made an unfair division of the spoils and of having appropriated the great bronze gates of Veii. Seeing that he would certainly
be condemned, he went into exile, whence he was recalled the next year
and made dictator against the Gauls.

267. *The Tribunes.* The tribunes of the people (*tribuni plebis*) were
first appointed in 494 B.C. after the first Secession to the Sacred Mount.
At first there were two tribunes ; afterwards the number was increased to
five, and finally to ten. They were originally appointed to afford protection to the common people against any abuse on the part of the patrician
magistrates ; and that they might be able to afford such protection, their
persons were declared sacred and inviolable. They gradually acquired the
right of vetoing any act which a magistrate might undertake during his
term of office, and that, too, without giving any reason. Moreover, they
might seize and imprison a senator or consul, or even hurl him from the
Tarpeian rock (see on 122 above). They convoked the assembly of the
tribes (*comitia tributa*), and usually presided over it. They finally became
the most powerful magistrates in the state, and in the latter days of the
republic were veritable tyrants. But in spite of the many abuses of
power by individual tribunes, the best historians and statesmen agree
that the greatness of Rome and its long duration were largely attributa-
ble to the institution of this office.

274. *Harness.* An old use of the word (which is cognate with *iron*)
in the sense of armor for the body. See Shakespeare, *T. and C.* v. 3.
31 : "Doff thy harness."

277. *Commons.* The plebeians or common people of Rome. The time
when they began to form part of the Roman population is uncertain, but
their number was greatly increased by the transfer to Rome of the population of Alba Longa, after that city was destroyed by Tullus Hostilius.
At first the plebeians were grievously oppressed by the patricians ; they
were denied all political rights, could not intermarry with the patricians,
and were subject to severe and unjust laws concerning debt. For about
two centuries the internal history of Rome is a record of the struggle between the two orders. Finally, after several secessions to the Sacred
Mount (see on *Lake Regillus,* 14 below) the Hortensian law in 286 B.C.
gave the plebeians equal rights with the patricians.

278. *Crow.* A bar with a strong beak like a crow's, a crow-bar.

PLEBEIANS.

290. *Rolled.* The verb (which somebody has criticised) is suggested by the *sea* above.

301. *Aunus.* This name does not occur anywhere in Roman literature.

Tifernum. There were two towns in Umbria by this name. The most important, and the one probably referred to here, was *Tifernum Tiberinum*, situated on the Tiber near the Tuscan frontier. The Tuscan villa of the younger Pliny was situated near Tifernum, whose citizens chose him at a very early age to be their patron ; in return for which honor he built a temple there.

303. *Seius.* There were several Romans of this name. Of one Gellius relates (iii. 9) that he had the finest horse of his age, which was fated to bring destruction to whosoever possessed it. Seius was put to death by M. Antonius, afterwards triumvir, during the civil war between Cæsar and Pompey. The horse then passed into the hands of Dolabella, and afterwards into those of Crassus, both of whom died a violent death. Hence the proverb concerning an unlucky man : " Ille homo habet equum Seianum."

304. *Ilva.* An island (now *Elba*) in the Tyrrhenian sea, situated off the coast of Etruria opposite Populonia (see on 30 above). It is about eighteen miles in length and twelve in breadth. It is still celebrated, as it was in ancient times, for its iron mines, the ore from which was very abundant and easily extracted.

305. *Picus.* The first king of Italy is said to have had this name.

309. *Nequinum.* The name applied before the Roman conquest to *Narnia*, one of the most important cities of Umbria, situated on the *Nar*, eight miles above its junction with the Tiber. It was on the Via Flaminia, fifty-six miles from Rome. Narnia was occupied by the generals of Vitellus in his civil war with Vespasian, and was an important fortress in the Gothic wars of Belisarius and Narses. The position of the town on a lofty hill, precipitous on several sides, and half surrounded by the Nar, is alluded to by many Latin writers ; and the bridge by which the Flaminian Way was carried across the Nar and a neighboring ravine at this point has been much admired in ancient and in modern times.

310. *Nar.* A river of central Italy, one of the principal tributaries of the Tiber, rising on the boundaries of Umbria and Picenum. It is remarkable for its white and sulphurous waters, which several ancient writers allude to. See Virgil, *Æneid*, vii. 517 :

> "Audiit amnis
> Sulfurea Nar albus aqua."

314. *Clove.* The form *cleft* is now more common for the past tense than *clove.* Shakespeare uses the former twice, the latter only once. He also has the participle *cleft* oftener than *cloven*, the latter being always joined to a noun ; as in *Tempest*, i. 2. 277 : "A cloven pine," etc.

319. *Ocnus.* The reputed founder of Mantua bore this name.

Falerii. A powerful city in the southern part of Etruria, a few miles north of Mt. Soracte. It was probably one of the twelve cities of the Etruscan League. It supported Veii in many of its wars with Rome ; and it is in connection with Falerii that the well-known story is told of the treacherous schoolmaster and the generous conduct of the Roman general.

321. *Lausulus.* There was a *Lausus* who was the son of Numitor, and another who was the son of Mezentius, slain by Æneas.

Urgo. A small island in the Tyrrhenian Sea, also called *Gorgon* (in modern times, *Gorgona*). It was between Etruria and Corsica, about twenty miles from the mainland. It is only eight miles in circumference, but elevated and rocky, so that it is conspicuous from a distance.

323. *Aruns.* An Etruscan designation of the younger son (in pure Etruscan, *Arnth*), while the elder was called *Lar.*

Volsinium (more properly *Volsinii*) was a city of Etruria on a steep height above the Volsinian lake (see on 49 above), and belonged to the Confederation. It was destroyed by the Romans, who compelled the inhabitants to migrate to the plain. This Roman Volsinii (the modern *Bolsena*) was the birthplace of Sejanus, the minister and favorite of Tiberius.

324. *Who slew the great wild boar.* Pliny (ii. 54) says that during the

reign of Porsena the country about Volsinii was ravaged by a monster called *Volta*, and that lightning was drawn down from heaven by Porsena to destroy it.

326. *Cosa.* A seaport of Etruria, on the remarkable promontory of Mons Argentarius (*Monte Argentaro*), whence Tacitus speaks of it as "Cosa, a promontory of Etruria." The remains of Cosa (about four miles from the modern *Orbetello*) are of much interest, and present an excellent specimen of ancient fortifications. The walls, nearly a mile in circuit, with their towers, are admirably preserved.

328. *Albinia.* A river of Etruria, the modern *Albegna*, flowing into the sea near Mons Argentarius. It is the same as the *Alminia* or *Almina*.

337. *Campania.* A province of Central Italy, bounded on the north by Latium, on the east by the mountains of Samnium, on the south by Lucania, and on the west by the Tyrrhenian Sea. It was noted for its fertility, the beauty of its sea-coast, and its soft and genial climate. Its shores also abounded in hot-springs, especially at Puteoli (the modern *Pozzuoli*), Baiæ, and Neapolis (*Naples*), and were much frequented by the Romans.

Hinds. Peasants, so called as belonging to the household or *hive* (a related word). The *d* is no part of the original word, and the form *hine* occurs in Chaucer.

350. *Luna.* See on 62 above.

360. *The she-wolf's litter.* Alluding to the familiar legend that Romulus and Remus, after being exposed for death by Amulius, were suckled by a she-wolf. Cf. Tennyson, *Princess*, vii. 113 :

> "By axe and eagle sat,
> With all their foreheads drawn in Roman scowls,
> And half the wolf's milk curdled in their veins,
> The fierce triumvirs."

Also Byron, *Childe Harold*, iv. 88 (referring to the bronze "Wolf of the Capitol") :

> "And thou, the thunder-stricken * nurse of Rome,
> She-wolf! whose brazen-imaged dugs impart
> The milk of conquest yet within the dome
> Where, as a monument of antique art,
> Thou standest," etc.

The first reading of lines 360, 361 (see Trevelyan's *Life*, vol. ii. p. 108) was :

> "By heaven," he said, "yon rebels
> Stand manfully at bay."

Mr. Ellis criticised "rebels," and Macaulay agreed with him that the word was "objectionable." See on 200 above.

369. *Deftly.* Neatly, dexterously. Cf. *Macbeth*, iv. 1. 68 : "Thyself and office deftly show."

---

* This statue (see cut on p. 106 above) is believed by some antiquarians to be the one referred to by Cicero (*Orat. in Catilinam,* iii. 8) as having been struck by lightning.

379. *Sped.* Sent, drove. On the passage, see p. 34 above.

384. *Mount Alvernus.* The modern *Alvernia,* or *La Vernia,* the height between the sources of the Tiber and the Arno, referred to by Dante, *Paradiso,* xi. 106: " Nel crudo sasso intra Tevere ed Arno." On its south-west slope, 3900 feet above the sea, is the famous monastery founded by St. Francis of Assisi in 1218.

388. *Augurs.* Strictly diviners by *birds* (from *avis* and a Sanscrit root *gar*), but in course of time the word was used in a more extended sense. At Rome the augurs were a college of priests, who made known the future by observing the lightning, the flight of birds, the feeding of the sacred fowls, certain appearances of quadrupeds, and any unusual occurrences. All important acts were preceded by consultation of the augurs. See Virgil, *Æneid,* i. 345: "primisque iugarat Ominibus ;" and Cicero, *In Catilinam,* iv. 2: "non campus, consularibus auspiciis consecratus." Cf. also *Virginia,* 151 below.

477. *Constant.* Firm, steadfast. Cf. Shakespeare, *Tempest,* i. 2. 207:

> " Who was so firm, so constant, that this coil
> Would not infect his reason?"

482. *Now yield thee,* etc. Professor John Wilson, of Edinburgh ("Macaulay's ancient adversary," as Trevelyan calls him), in a review of the *Lays* in *Blackwood* (vol. 52, p. 812) remarks: " Porsena was a noble personage, and he 'shines well where he stands' throughout the ballad. Much is made of his power and state on the march, for he knew what kind of city he sought to storm. But his magnanimity is grandly displayed by his behavior at the bridge—in contrast with the false Sextus, cruel and pusillanimous ever."

483. *Our grace.* Our mercy, or the *grace* (favor) we may show thee. Cf. *3 Hen. VI.* ii. 2. 81: " Now perjur'd Henry, wilt thou kneel for grace ?"

488. *Palatinus.* One of the seven hills of Rome. It was the hill first settled, and so was the cradle of Rome, as well as the seat of her matured power. In the time of Horatius the dwellings of the principal patricians stood there, while in later times it was the residence of the Roman emperors, " ipsa imperii arx," as Tacitus (*Hist.* iii. 70) calls it. From *Palatinus* for this reason is derived the English word *palace.*

492. *Father Tiber.* The Romans generally believed that the Tiber was originally called *Albula* (as it was often designated by the poets), but that it changed its name because Tiberinus, one of the fabulous kings of Alba, was drowned in its waters. Virgil, however, who calls the king *Thybris,* assigns him to a period before the landing of Æneas (*Æneid,* viii. 330). As Cicero tells us, it had its tutelary divinity, *Tiberinus,* who was invoked by the augurs in their prayers, and whom the poets call " Pater Tiberinus." See cut on p. 39 above.

511. *Swollen high by months of rain.* Floods of the Tiber, which did much damage, were a common occurrence, as in more recent times. The earliest recorded, in 241 B.C., is said to have swept away all the houses and buildings in the lower part of the city. Great attention was given to the subject by Augustus, and he first instituted magistrates, called *Cu-*

'read before,' that very instant they drop it, as if their hand were stung. Why, Sir Walter kept reciting his favorite old ballads almost every day in his life for forty years, and with the same fire about his eyes, till even they grew dim at last. He would have rejoiced in *Horatius,* as if he had been a doughty Douglas. We have read it till we find we have got it by heart, and, as our memory is nothing remarkable, all the syllables must have gone six times through our sensorium."

THE BATTLE OF THE LAKE REGILLUS.

Macaulay's introduction to the poem is as follows:

" The following poem is supposed to have been produced about ninety years after the lay of *Horatius.* Some persons mentioned in the lay of *Horatius* make their appearance again, and some appellations and epithets used in the lay of *Horatius* have been purposely repeated; for, in an age of ballad-poetry, it scarcely ever fails to happen that certain phrases come to be appropriated to certain men and things, and are regularly applied to those men and things by every minstrel. Thus we find, both in the Homeric poems and in Hesiod, βίη Ἡρακληείη, περικλύτος Ἀμφιγυήεις, διάκτορος Ἀργειφόντης, ἑπτάπυλος Θήβη, Ἑλένης ἕνεκ' ἠϋκόμοιο. Thus, too, in our own national songs, Douglas is almost always the doughty Douglas; England is merry England; all the gold is red; and all the ladies are gay.

" The principal distinction between the lay of *Horatius* and the lay of the *Lake Regillus* is that the former is meant to be purely Roman, while the latter, though national in its general spirit, has a slight tincture of Greek learning and of Greek superstition. The story of the Tarquins, as it has come down to us, appears to have been compiled from the works of several popular poets; and one, at least, of those poets appears to have visited the Greek colonies in Italy, if not Greece itself, and to have had some acquaintance with the works of Homer and Herodotus. Many of the most striking adventures of the House of Tarquin, before Lucretia makes her appearance, have a Greek character. The Tarquins themselves are represented as Corinthian nobles of the great House of the Bacchiadæ, driven from their country by the tyranny of that Cypselus the tale of whose strange escape Herodotus has related with incomparable simplicity and liveliness.* Livy and Dionysius tell us that, when Tarquin the Proud was asked what was the best mode of governing a conquered city, he replied only by beating down with his staff all the tallest poppies in his garden.† This is exactly what Herodotus, in the passage to which reference has already been made, relates of the counsel given to Periander, the son of Cypselus. The stratagem by which the town of Gabii is brought under the power of the Tarquins is, again, obviously copied from Herodotus.‡ The embassy of the young Tarquins to the

---

* Herodotus, v. 92; Livy, v. i. 34; Dionysius, iii. 46.
† Livy, i. 51; Dionysius, iv. 56.
‡ Herodotus, iii. 154; Livy, i. 53.

oracle at Delphi is just such a story as would be told by a poet whose head was full of the Greek mythology ; and the ambiguous answer returned by Apollo is in the exact style of the prophecies which, according to Herodotus, lured Crœsus to destruction. Then the character of the narrative changes. From the first mention of Lucretia to the retreat of Porsena nothing seems to be borrowed from foreign sources. The villany of Sextus, the suicide of his victim, the revolution, the death of the sons of Brutus, the defence of the bridge, Mucius burning his hand,* Clœlia swimming through Tiber, seem to be all strictly Roman. But when we have done with the Tuscan war, and enter upon the war with the Latines, we are again struck by the Greek air of the story. The Battle of the Lake Regillus is, in all respects, a Homeric battle, except that the combatants ride astride on their horses, instead of driving chariots. The mass of fighting-men is hardly mentioned. The leaders single each other out, and engage hand to hand. The great object of the warriors on both sides is, as in the Iliad, to obtain possession of the spoils and bodies of the slain ; and several circumstances are related which forcibly remind us of the great slaughter round the corpses of Sarpedon and Patroclus.

"But there is one circumstance which deserves especial notice. Both the war of Troy and the war of Regillus were caused by the licentious passions of young princes, who were therefore peculiarly bound not to be sparing of their own persons in the day of battle. Now the conduct of Sextus at Regillus, as described by Livy, so exactly resembles that of Paris, as described at the beginning of the third book of the Iliad, that it is difficult to believe the resemblance accidental. Paris appears before the Trojan ranks, defying the bravest Greek to encounter him.

> Τρωσὶν μὲν προμάχιζεν Ἀλέξανδρος θεοειδής,
> . . . Ἀργείων προκαλίζετο πάντας ἀρίστους,
> ἀντίβιον μαχέσασθαι ἐν αἰνῇ δηϊοτῆτι.

Livy introduces Sextus in a similar manner : 'Ferocem juvenem Tarquinium, ostentantem se in prima exsulum acie.' Menelaus rushes to meet Paris. A Roman noble, eager for vengeance, spurs his horse towards Sextus. Both the guilty princes are instantly terror-stricken :

> Τὸν δ' ὡς οὖν ἐνόησεν Ἀλέξανδρος θεοειδὴς
> ἐν προμάχοισι φανέντα, κατεπλήγη φίλον ἦτορ·
> ἂψ δ' ἑτάρων εἰς ἔθνος ἐχάζετο κῆρ' ἀλεείνων.

'Tarquinius,' says Livy, 'retro in agmen suorum infenso cessit hosti.' If this be a fortuitous coincidence, it is one of the most extraordinary in literature.

"In the following poem, therefore, images and incidents have been borrowed, not merely without scruple, but on principle, from the incomparable battle-pieces of Homer.

"The popular belief at Rome, from an early period, seems to have

---

* M. de Pouilly attempted, a hundred and twenty years ago, to prove that the story of Mucius was of Greek origin ; but he was signally confuted by the Abbé Sallier. See the *Mémoires de l'Académie des Inscriptions*, vi. 27, 66.

been that the event of the great day of Regillus was decided by super-natural agency. Castor and Pollux, it was said, had fought, armed and mounted, at the head of the legions of the Commonwealth, and had after-wards carried the news of the victory with incredible speed to the city. The well in the Forum at which they had alighted was pointed out. Near the well rose their ancient temple. A great festival was kept to their honor on the ides of Quintilis, supposed to be the anniversary of the bat-tle ; and on that day sumptuous sacrifices were offered to them at the public charge. One spot on the margin of Lake Regillus was regarded during many ages with superstitious awe. A mark, resembling in shape a horse's hoof, was discernible in the volcanic rock ; and this mark was believed to have been made by one of the celestial chargers.

"How the legend originated cannot now be ascertained ; but we may easily imagine several ways in which it might have originated ; nor is it at all necessary to suppose, with Julius Frontinus, that two young men were dressed up by the Dictator to personate the sons of Leda. It is probable that Livy is correct when he says that the Roman general, in the hour of peril, vowed a temple to Castor. If so, nothing could be more natural than that the multitude should ascribe the victory to the favor of the Twin Gods. When such was the prevailing sentiment, any man who chose to declare that, in the midst of the confusion and slaugh-ter, he had seen two godlike forms on white horses scattering the Latines would find ready credence. We know, indeed, that, in modern times, a very similar story actually found credence among a people much more civilized than the Romans of the fifth century before Christ. A chaplain of Cortes, writing about thirty years after the conquest of Mexico, in an age of printing-presses, libraries, universities, scholars, logicians, jurists, and statesmen, had the face to assert that, in one engagement against the Indians, Saint James had appeared on a gray horse at the head of the Castilian adventurers. Many of those adventurers were living when this lie was printed. One of them, honest Bernal Diaz, wrote an account of the expedition. He had the evidence of his own senses against the legend ; but he seems to have distrusted even the evidence of his own senses. He says that he was in the battle, and that he saw a gray horse with a man on his back, but the man was, to his thinking, Francisco de Morla, and not the ever-blessed apostle Saint James. 'Nevertheless,' Bernal adds, 'it may be that the person on the gray horse was the glori-ous apostle Saint James, and that I, sinner that I am, was unworthy to see him.' The Romans of the age of Cincinnatus were probably quite as credulous as the Spanish subjects of Charles the Fifth. It is therefore conceivable that the appearance of Castor and Pollux may have become an article of faith before the generation which had fought at Regillus had passed away. Nor could anything be more natural than that the poets of the next age should embellish this story, and make the celestial horse-men bear the tidings of victory to Rome.

"Many years after the temple of the Twin Gods had been built in the Forum, an important addition was made to the ceremonial by which the state annually testified its gratitude for their protection. Quintus Fabius and Publius Decius were elected censors at a momentous crisis. It had

10

become absolutely necessary that the classification of the citizens should be revised. On that classification depended the distribution of political power. Party-spirit ran high ; and the Republic seemed to be in danger of falling under the dominion either of a narrow oligarchy or of an ignorant and headstrong rabble. Under such circumstances, the most illustrious patrician and the most illustrious plebeian of the age were intrusted with the office of arbitrating between the angry factions ; and they performed their arduous task to the satisfaction of all honest and reasonable men.

"One of their reforms was a remodelling of the equestrian order ; and, having effected this reform, they determined to give to their work a sanction derived from religion. In the chivalrous societies of modern times —societies which have much more than may at first sight appear in common with the equestrian order of Rome—it has been usual to invoke the special protection of some saint, and to observe his day with peculiar solemnity. Thus the Companions of the Garter wear the image of Saint George depending from their collars, and meet, on great occasions, in Saint George's Chapel. Thus, when Louis the Fourteenth instituted a new order of chivalry for the rewarding of military merit, he commended it to the favor of his own glorified ancestor and patron, and decreed that all the members of the fraternity should meet at the royal palace on the feast of Saint Louis, should attend the king to chapel, should hear mass, and should subsequently hold their great annual assembly. There is a considerable resemblance between this rule of the Order of Saint Louis and the rule which Fabius and Decius made respecting the Roman knights. It was ordained that a grand muster and inspection of the equestrian body should be part of the ceremonial performed, on the anniversary of the battle of Regillus, in honor of Castor and Pollux, the two equestrian gods. All the knights, clad in purple and crowned with olive, were to meet at a temple of Mars in the suburbs. Thence they were to ride in state to the Forum, where the temple of the Twins stood. This pageant was, during several centuries, considered as one of the most splendid sights of Rome. In the time of Dionysius the cavalcade sometimes consisted of five thousand horsemen, all persons of fair repute and easy fortune.*

"There can be no doubt that the censors who instituted this august ceremony acted in concert with the pontiffs, to whom, by the constitution of Rome, the superintendence of the public worship belonged ; and it is probable that those high religious functionaries were, as usual, fortunate enough to find in their books or traditions some warrant for the innovation.

"The following poem is supposed to have been made for this great occasion. Songs, we know, were chanted at the religious festivals of Rome from an early period, indeed from so early a period that some of the sacred verses were popularly ascribed to Numa, and were utterly un-

---

* See Livy, ix. 46 ; Val. Max. ii. 2 ; Aurel. Vict. *De Viris Illustribus*, 32 ; Dionysius, vi. 13 ; Plin. *Hist. Nat.* xv. 5. See also the singularly ingenious chapter in Niebuhr's posthumous volume, *Die Censur des Q. Fabius und P. Decius.*

intelligible in the age of Augustus. In the Second Punic war, a great feast was held in honor of Juno, and a song was sung in her praise. This song was extant when Livy wrote, and, though exceedingly rugged and uncouth, seemed to him not wholly destitute of merit.* A song, as we learn from Horace,† was part of the established ritual at the great Secular Jubilee. It is therefore likely that the censors and pontiffs, when they had resolved to add a grand procession of knights to the other solemnities annually performed on the ides of Quintilis, would call in the aid of a poet. Such a poet would naturally take for his subject the battle of Regillus, the appearance of the Twin Gods, and the institution of their festival. He would find abundant materials in the ballads of his predecessors; and he would make free use of the scanty stock of Greek learning which he had himself acquired. He would probably introduce some wise and holy pontiff enjoining the magnificent ceremonial which, after a long interval, had at length been adopted. If the poem succeeded, many persons would commit it to memory. Parts of it would be sung to the pipe at banquets. It would be peculiarly interesting to the great Posthumian House, which numbered among its many images that of the Dictator Aulus, the hero of Regillus. The orator who, in the following generation, pronounced the funeral panegyric over the remains of Lucius Posthumius Magellus, thrice Consul, would borrow largely from the lay; and thus some passages, much disfigured, would probably find their way into the chronicles which were afterwards in the hands of Dionysius and Livy.

" Antiquaries differ widely as to the situation of the field of battle. The opinion of those who suppose that the armies met near Cornufelle, between Frascati and the Monte Porzio, is at least plausible, and has been followed in the poem.

" As to the details of the battle, it has not been thought desirable to adhere minutely to the accounts which have come down to us. Those accounts, indeed, differ widely from each other, and, in all probability, differ as widely from the ancient poem from which they were originally derived.

" It is unnecessary to point out the obvious imitations of the Iliad, which have been purposely introduced."

2. *Lictors.* Public officers who attended the chief Roman magistrates, as a sign of official dignity. They bore a bundle of rods called *fasces*, from which an axe projected. Their duty was to walk before the magistrates in line, to call out to the people to make way, and to serve as a bodyguard. They also executed judicial sentences. In the earliest times the kings had twelve lictors. After the expulsion of the kings, each consul had twelve, but it was soon decreed that they should be preceded for a month by twelve in turn. By a law of Valerius Publicola (see on 376 below) the axes were removed when the consuls were in the city. The prætors were preceded by six lictors. Hence Cicero, when speaking of the capture of two prætors by the pirates, says (*De Lege Manilia*, 12. 32):

---

* Livy, xxvii. 97. † Horace, *Carmen Sæculare.*

"Cum duodecim secures in praedonum potestatem pervenerint."

3. *The knights will ride in all their pride*, etc. The knights (*equites*) were originally the cavalry of the state, who received a horse and a sum of money for its annual support. To serve *equo publico* one must have a fortune of not less than 400,000 asses, and the horses were usually assigned to young men of senatorial families. There were but six centuries of equites up to the time of Servius Tullius, who added twelve more; and these eighteen equestrian centuries afterwards remained a distinct class. They ceased to serve in the field at an early period, their place being taken by foreign cavalry, Gauls, Numidians, etc.

At the time of the siege of Veii (403 B.C.) a second class of equites arose, who, although having a property of 400,000 asses, had to furnish their

LICTORS.

own horses. They were mostly wealthy young men of non-senatorial families, and were not included in the eighteen equestrian centuries. From this last class of equites (*equites privato equo*) grew up in later times the *Equestrian Order*, a moneyed aristocracy occupying a position in the state between the nobility (see on *Horatius*, 138 above) and the common people. The members of the equestrian order wore a narrow purple stripe on the tunic and a gold ring (which was originally the badge of the *equites equo publico*), and the first fourteen rows of seats in the theatre behind the orchestra were given to them.

Every year on the ides of Quintilis (July) the *Equitum Transvectio* took place, the solemn procession to the institution of which Macaulay refers on p. 146 above. On this occasion the equites were not only crowned with olive, but they also wore their insignia of rank and deeds. According to Dionysius this procession was instituted after the battle of Lake Regillus.

7. *Castor in the Forum*. The temple of Castor. Cf. Horace, *Satires*, i. 9. 35 : "Ventum erat ad Vestae," that is to the temple (or, as some authorities say, to the *Atrium*) of Vesta; and see 745 below. This temple was one of the earliest buildings erected in the forum. It was dedicated in 484 B.C. to commemorate the event which is the subject of this poem. It served for assemblies of the senate and for judicial business. Its importance is spoken of by Cicero, *In Verrem*, i. 49. Although dedicated to the Twin Gods, it was commonly called only *Ædes Castoris;* on which account Bibulus, the colleague of Cæsar in his ædileship, compared himself with Pollux, who, though he shared the temple in common with his brother, was never once named. The temple was rebuilt by Quintus Me-

tellus, 119 B.C., and again by Tiberius, who dedicated it in his own name and that of his brother Drusus. Caligula broke through the rear wall and connected the temple with his palace on the Palatine; and he is said to have sometimes exhibited himself for adoration between the statues of the twin deities. Three elegant Corinthian columns remain to mark the site of this temple.

The word *forum* signifies an open place, and seems to be connected with the adverb *foras*. The *Forum Romanum*, the principal and at first the only forum at Rome, was situated between the Palatine and Capitoline hills. It was used originally as a place for the administration of justice, for holding the assemblies of the people, and for transacting other kinds of public business. In its widest sense it included the *comitium* (see on *Horatius*, 550 above). It was surrounded by temples and public buildings, whose porticoes were favorite lounging-places (see on *Virginia*, 419 below).

8. *Mars without the wall.* The temple of Mars, just outside the Porta Capena. Cf. Ovid, *Fasti*, vi. 191 :

> " Lux eadem Marti festa est; quam prospicit extra
> Appositum Tectae Porta Capena viae."

No trace now remains of the edifice, nor of the temples of Hercules, of Honor, and of Virtue, which were near it. The route of the military procession on the anniversary of the Battle of Lake Regillus was as here described by Macaulay. Cf. 788 below.

13. *The Yellow River.* See on *Horatius*, 98 above.

14. *The Sacred Hill.* The Sacred Mount, just outside the city, to which the plebeians made several secessions during their struggles with the patricians. The first secession, in 494 B.C., resulted in the creation of the office of tribune.

15. *The ides of Quintilis.* The fifteenth day of July. The ides were the fifteenth of March, May, July, and October, and the thirteenth of the other months. July and August were originally called Quintilis and Sextilis, the fifth and sixth months (counting from March), but afterwards received their present names in honor of Julius and Augustus Cæsar.

17. *The Martian calends.* On the calends, or first, of March was celebrated the *Matronalia*, or the feast of married persons in honor of Juno Lucina (see on *Horatius*, 562 above). See Horace, *Odes*, iii. 8. 1:

> " Martiis caelebs quid agam Kalendis,
> Quid velint flores et acerra thuris
> Plena, miraris, positusque carbo in
> Caespite vivo,
> Docte sermones utriusque linguae ?"

Juvenal (ix. 53) calls it "femineas Kalendas." It seems to have been instituted in memory of the peace between the Romans and the Sabines, which was brought about by the Sabine women. Presents were given by husbands to their wives, and female slaves were feasted by their mistresses ; hence it is called by Martial the Saturnalia of women. The great feast of Mars (see on *Horatius*, 81 above) occurred on the same day.

18. *December's nones.* The nones were the seventh of March, May, July, and October, and the fifth of the other months. The word is derived from *nonus* (ninth), because, by the peculiar Roman method of inclusive reckoning, the nones were the ninth day before the ides. The reference is to the *Faunalia*, or festival in honor of Faunus. See Horace, *Odes*, iii. 18. 10.

20. *Rome's whitest day.* That is, its most propitious day. Cf. 156 and 780 below, where there is an allusion to the Roman custom of marking lucky days with a white stone, as unlucky ones were marked with black. Cf. Tibullus, iii. 630: "O me felicem, O nox mihi candida !" Horace, *Satires*, ii. 3. 246 : "Sanin creta an carbone notandi ?" Id. *Odes*, i. 12. 27 : "simul alba nautis Stella refulsit ;" Persius, *Satires*, i. 110 : "Sed current albusque dies horaeque serenae," etc.

25. *Parthenius.* A mountain, about 4000 feet high, on the frontiers of Arcadia and Argolis, across which there was an important pass leading from Argos to Tegea. The mountain was sacred to Pan. The pass still bears the name of *Parthéni*, but the mountain is called *Róino.*

27. *Cirrha.* A very ancient town of Phocis, near Delphi, devoted to Apollo. Near the city lay a fertile plain. After the Sacred War, 595 B.C., waged against the Cirrhæans by the Amphictyons, Cirrha was destroyed, the plain was dedicated to the god, and a curse was imprecated on any one who should till or dwell upon it. In the time of Philip I. of Macedon, the Amphissians dared to cultivate the sacred plain and to rebuild the city. This led to the Second Sacred War, 338 B.C. Cirrha was near the Homeric Crissa, with which it has been sometimes confounded, as by Pausanias (x. 37. 5). It is Crissa which was situated on a height, a spur of Mount Parnassus. Cirrha grew up afterwards at the base of the hill. Our author seems to look on the two towns as one and the same.

Adria. Poetical name for the Adriatic. Cf. 653 below ; and see on *Virginia*, 551. The Latin name was *Adria*, or more properly *Hadria*. Cf. Byron, *Don Juan :* "The song and oar of Adria's gondolier."

28. *Apennine.* The singular is according to the Latin usage. The Romans called the chain *Mons Apenninus.* Cf. Byron, *Childe Harold*, iv. 73 :

> "Once more upon the woody Apennine,
>   The infant Alps."

31. *Lacedæmon.* Or Sparta, the famous capital of Laconia, on the Eurotas. The *Dioscuri* (Castor and Pollux) were the sons of Leda and Tyndareus, king of Lacedæmon, and brothers of Helen and Clytemnestra.

32. *The city of two kings.* From the earliest times the Lacedæmonians were governed by two kings. This custom is said to have arisen from the fact that Aristodemus, one of the Heraclidæ, who, according to the myth, overran the Peloponnesus, had twin sons.

33. *Lake Regillus.* A small lake in Latium, at the foot of the Tusculan hills. See Macaulay's introduction to the poem above. On the whole, the lake (now dried up) is more likely to have been in the broad plain to the north of the "Porcian height," between the ancient Gabii and the modern town of Colonna.

34. *The Porcian height.* M. Porcius Cato, among other distinguished Romans, had a villa northeast of Tusculum, on a hill which seems thence to have got the name of *Mons Porcius* (now *Monte Porzio*).

35. *Tusculum.* See on *Horatius*, 96 above.

37-40. *Now on the place of slaughter*, etc. With this description c. the present peaceful aspect of a battle-field, cf. Byron, *Childe Harold*, iv. 65:

> "Far other scene is Trasimene now;
> Her lake a sheet of silver, and her plain
> Rent by no ravage save the gentle plow;
> Her aged trees rise thick as once the slain
> Lay where their roots are."

42. *Corne's oaks.* Pliny (*Nat. Hist.* xvi. 92) describes a hill called *Corne* in this part of Italy, whereon there was a grove of beeches, one of which, remarkable for its size, was so much admired by Passienus, the orator and consul, that he used to embrace it, sleep under it, and pour wine upon it. Near this grove was a holm-oak (*ilex*) so large that, as Pliny says, it was a forest of itself (*silvamque sola facit*).

43. *The Fair Fount.* Evidently a fountain in the same vicinity, but we have not met with any reference to it in the authorities.

45. *Angle.* A fishing-hook (A. S. *angel*). Cf. the Latin *uncus*, and the Greek ὄγκος, ἀγκών.

63. *What time.* At the time when; used only in poetry. Cf. Milton, *Lycidas*, 28: "What time the gray-fly winds her sultry horn," etc.

The Thirty Cities. Pliny tells us that there were thirty towns or communities which were accustomed to share in sacrifices on the Alban Mount; and this number seems to have been a recognized and established one, for the Latin League which entered into an alliance with Rome in 493 B.C. also consisted of thirty cities, of which a list is given by Dionysius.

69. *A hoof-mark.* See Macaulay's introduction, p. 145 above.

81. *Virginius.* The first of the *Virginia gens* to be consul was T. Virginius Tricostus Cæliomontanus, in 496 B.C.

82. *Was Consul first in place.* The two consuls had equal rights in all respects. Virginius was merely the first to obtain a majority in the comitia. Cf. Cicero, *Pro Lege Manilia*, 1. 2: "Cum propter dilationem comitiorum ter praetor primus centuriis cunctis renuntiatus sum."

84. *Posthumian race.* The proper spelling is *Postumian.* The first of the *gens* to be consul was P. Postumius Tubertus in 503 B.C. *Albus* was the name of the principal family of the *gens*. A. Postumius Albus Regillensis was consul 496 B.C. and dictator in 498 B.C. when the battle of Lake Regillus is said to have been fought. His surname was probably not derived from the battle, as Livy (xxx. 45) expressly states that Scipio Africanus was the first Roman who obtained a surname from his conquests.

86. *Gabii.* An ancient city of Latium situated about twelve miles from Rome on the road to Præneste. It was one of the largest and most populous of the cities of the Latin league. It was captured when Tarquin the Proud was king of Rome by a stratagem of his son Sextus. Afterwards,

however, it combined with the other cities of Latium in his behalf against Rome. Gabii had fallen into decline in Cicero's time, but revived during the Empire. It lay close to a small volcanic lake, now drained, which, strangely enough, is not mentioned by any writer before the 5th century.

92. *A sceptre.* This word originally meant a staff to lean upon, not a symbol of station or authority. Sceptres were carried by kings, princes, and leaders ; also by judges, heralds (as here), priests, and seers.

105. *Eyry.* The more proper spelling of this word is *aery*, which occurs in Shakespeare, *K. John*, v. 2. 149, and *Hamlet*, ii. 2. 354. It is cognate with the Greek ὄρνις and ὀρνύναι and the Latin *oriri*. "When fairly imported into English, the word was ingeniously connected with *ey*, an egg, as if the word meant an *eggery ;* hence it began to be spelled *eyrie* or *eyry*, and to be misinterpreted accordingly" (Skeat).

119. *Conscript Fathers.* *Patres Conscripti* (see on *Horatius*, 126 above) ; originally *Patres et Conscripti*, the latter being certain noble plebeians of equestrian rank added to the senate when its numbers had fallen off, in the early days of the Republic. Some authorities, however, make *Patres Conscripti* = enrolled fathers.

123. *Choose we a Dictator.* Let us choose (1st person imperative) a dictator. The dictator was an extraordinary magistrate appointed in time of peril. As indicated below, he held his office for six months only, was preceded by twenty-four lictors (see on 2 above) with the *fasces* and axes, and had associated with him a lieutenant, called the master of horse (*magister equitum*), usually appointed by himself, but sometimes by the senate. The dictator was appointed by a decree of the senate on the nomination of the consul. He had greater power than the consul in that he had no colleague, was more independent of the senate, had greater freedom of punishment without appeal, and was irresponsible. The first dictator was appointed in 501 B.C., and the office disappeared in 202 B.C.; for the dictatorships of Sulla and Cæsar were of a different character. After that date, however, the consuls were given dictatorial power by the senate in times of danger, by the common formula, "Consul videat ne quid res publica detrimenti capiat." Cf. Cicero, *In Catilinam*, i. 2. 4 : "Decrevit quondam senatus ut L. Opimius Consul videret ne quid res publica detrimenti caperet."

125. *Camerium.* An ancient city of Latium. It was taken by Tarquin during his reign, but after his expulsion from Rome it was among the first to embrace his cause, and was destroyed by Virginius, 502 B.C.

135. *Æbutius Elva.* Consul 497 B.C. He had charge of the city when the battle of Lake Regillus was fought.

143. *With boys*, etc. Cf. *Horatius*, 58 fol.

148. *The Porcian height.* See on 34 above.

156. *Marked evermore with white.* See on 20 above, and cf. 780 below.

165. *Setia.* An ancient city of Latium, on the southern slope of the Volscian mountains, looking over the Pomptine Marshes (see on 263 below). It was one of the thirty cities of the Latin League. It was a strong fortress during the wars of Marius and Sulla. It was noted for its wine, which in the days of Martial and Juvenal seems to have been considered one of the choicest kinds. According to Pliny (xiv. 6–8), Au-

gustus first brought it into vogue. There can be no doubt that the modern town of Sezza occupies the site of ancient Setia, as remnants of its
walls, built of large polygonal blocks of limestone, like those of Norba,
are still visible.

166. *Norba.* On the border of the Volscian mountains near Setia, and
one of the thirty cities of the Latin League. It was the last fortress of
Italy that held out against Sulla. His general, Lepidus, utterly destroyed
it, and it was never rebuilt. The existing ruins of Norba are among the
most perfect specimens remaining in Italy of the style of construction
known as Cyclopean.

167. *Tusculum.* See on *Horatius*, 96 above.

169. *The Witch's Fortress.* The Circæan promontory (*Monte Circello*),
on the coast of the Tyrrhenian Sea, which was supposed to have been
the abode of the enchantress Circe. It is a bold and abrupt mountain,
rising precipitously from the sea to the height of 1800 feet, and insulated
on the land side by a strip of the Pomptine Marshes.

172. *Aricia.* An ancient and famous city of Latium, on the Appian
Way, sixteen miles from Rome. It took a prominent part in this Latin
war. The modern town (*Ariccia*) occupies the site of the ancient citadel,
on a steep hill rising above a basin-shaped valley, evidently at one time
filled by a lake.

Aricia was celebrated throughout Italy for its temple of Diana, situated about three miles from the town on the edge of a small lake. It
was remarkable for the barbarous custom, retained even in the days of
Strabo and Pausanias, of having as high priest a fugitive slave, who had
obtained the office by killing his predecessor, for which reason the priests
always went armed. The lake (the modern *Lago di Nemi*) was often
called *Speculum Dianæ*, and is still noted for its beauty. Cf. Byron,
Childe Harold, iv. 172 :

> " Lo ! Nemi, navelled in the woody hills
> So far that the uprooting wind which tears
> The oak from its foundation, and which spills
> The ocean o'er its boundary and bears
> Its foam against the skies, reluctant spares
> The oval mirror of thy glassy lake;
> And, calm as cherished hate, its surface wears
> A deep, cold, settled aspect nought can shake,
> All coiled into itself and round, as sleeps the snake."

177. *Ufens.* A river of Latium, rising at the foot of the Volscian
mountains and flowing through the Pontine Marshes, whence it is described by Virgil (*Æneid*, vii. 801) as a sluggish, muddy stream.

183. *Cora.* A city of Latium (now *Cori*), on the left of the Appian Way
about thirty-seven miles from Rome. It stands on a bold hill on the out-
skirts of the Volscian mountains, and overlooks the Pontine Marshes,
the "never-ending fen." Its fortifications, apparently built at different
periods, formed three successive tiers, the uppermost of which enclosed
the highest summit of the hill and was the citadel of the ancient town.
Considerable portions of these walls, with other ruins of much interest,
are still to be seen.

LAKE OF NEMI, LOOKING OVER THE CAMPAGNA.

185. *The Laurentian jungle.* Laurentum, on the sea-coast between Ostia and Lavinium, was the ancient capital of Latium and the abode of King Latinus when Æneas landed. In its immediate neighborhood were considerable marshes, while a little farther inland stood the extensive Laurentian Forest. Under the Roman Empire this forest abounded in wild boars, which were of large size, but reckoned of inferior flavor on account of the marshy ground on which they fed. The orator Hortensius had a villa and a park stocked with game near Laurentum, and many villas lined the coast.

187. *Anio.* A celebrated river of Latium, in ancient times called the *Anien*, one of the largest tributaries of the Tiber. It is now called the *Teverone.* Near Tibur it forms a celebrated cascade, falling at once through a height of more than eighty feet. The present cascade is artificial, the waters of the river having been carried through a tunnel constructed for the purpose in 1834, but the Anio always formed a striking fall at this point. See Horace, *Odes,* i. 7. 13 : " Et praeceps Anio." The waters of the upper Anio were very clear, for which reason they were carried by aqueducts to Rome.

190. *Velitræ.* A city (now *Velletri*) on the southern slope of the Alban Hills, on the Via Appia, looking over the Pontine Marshes. Both Livy and Dionysius represent it as a Volscian city when it first came into collision with Rome, but Dionysius includes it among the thirty cities of

Latium. After the Latin war in 338 B.C., the walls of Velitræ were destroyed, and the town became an ordinary municipality. It was the native place of the Octavian family, from which Augustus was descended. Pliny mentions it as producing a wine inferior only to the Falernian.

193. *Mamilius.* See on *Horatius*, 96 above.

202. *By Syria's dark-browed daughters.* The finest purple robes came from Tyre in Phœnicia, on the coast of Syria.

203. *Carthage.* Situated on the northern coast of Africa near the modern Tunis. It was a Phœnician colony, founded, according to the popular chronology, 814 B.C., and destroyed after three wars with Rome in 146 B.C. It was rebuilt by Augustus and became one of the most flourishing cities of the ancient world. In the fifth century it was taken by the Vandals under Genseric, and became the capital of their kingdom in Africa. It was retaken by Belisarius, but was captured and destroyed by the Arabs in 647.

At the period of the poem Carthage was already a flourishing and wealthy commercial city, and the depot of supplies for the western Mediterranean of the products of the East. See on *The Prophecy of Capys*, 280 below.

205. *Lavinium.* A city about three miles from the sea-coast, between Laurentum and Ardea, and seventeen miles from Rome. It was founded, according to the legend, by Æneas, shortly after his landing in Italy, and named by him after his wife Lavinia, daughter of King Latinus. When Ascanius removed the seat of the government to Alba, the attempt to remove the Penates was unsuccessful; hence Lavinium was always regarded as a sacred metropolis. Macrobius tells us that in his time it was customary for the consuls and prætors, at the beginning of their term of office, to offer sacrifice there to Vesta and the Penates. While the legend of Æneas has no historical basis, it seems certain for many reasons, among them the name, that Lavinium was originally the capital of Latium. The insignificant village of *Practica* now occupies the site.

209. *False Sextus*, etc. See on *Horatius*, 199 above.

233. *Tibur.* The modern *Tivoli*, a town twenty miles northeast of Rome on the Anio. It was celebrated for its orchards and for its grapes and figs. Its air was healthy and bracing, and this, together with its beautiful scenery, made it a favorite resort of the wealthy Romans. It was much older than Rome, and probably of Greek origin. Here Syphax, king of Numidia, died 201 B.C., and here Zenobia lived as a captive. Tibur was famed for its worship of Hercules, whose temple was the most remarkable in the neighborhood of Rome, except that of Fortune at Præneste. Both Horace and Sallust had residences at Tibur.

Pedum. A city of the Latin League, at one time of considerable importance. It disappears from history after the close of the Latin War in 338 B.C.

235. *Ferentinum.* A city of Etruria about five miles from the Tiber on the north of the Ciminian range.

236. *Gabii.* See on 86 above.

237. *Volscian succors.* The Volscians (see on *Horatius*, 561 above) were usually opposed to the Latins, and in alliance with the Æquians.

Tarquinius Superbus is said to have built the Capitol at Rome from spoils taken from the Volscians, a tradition which proves the belief in their great wealth and power at this early period.

241. *Mount Soracte.* A mountain of Etruria (now called *Monte di San Oreste*), situated between Falerii and the Tiber, about twenty-six miles north of Rome. Although only 2260 feet in height, it rises in an abrupt mass above the plain, and is a conspicuous object in all views of the Campagna. See Horace, *Odes*, i. 9. 1 : "Vides ut alta stet nive candidum Soracte ;" and Virgil, *Æneid*, xi. 785 : "Summe deum, sancti custos Soractis Apollo."

250. *Apulian.* Apulia was a district in the southeastern part of Italy, between the Apennines and the sea. A great part of northern Apulia consisted of a fertile plain, especially adapted to the rearing of horses and cattle.

251. *Titus, the youngest Tarquin.* Titus was the eldest son of Tarquin. The youngest son was Aruns. See on *Horatius*, 323 above.

256. *Targe.* A poetical word for a small round shield. *Target* is a diminutive of it.

263. *Pomptine fog.* The Pomptine (Pontine) Marshes (*Pomptinae Paludes*) were an extensive tract of marshy ground in the south of Latium at the foot of the Volscian mountains. They occupy a space of thirty miles in length by seven or eight in breadth, and are separated from the sea on the west by a broad tract of sandy plain covered with forest, which is perfectly level and intermixed with marshy spots and pools of stagnant

THE PONTINE MARSHES.

water, so that it is almost as unhealthy as the Marshes proper, and is often included under the same name. The entire tract is of very recent origin as compared with the rest of the mainland. The Romans believed that the whole of this accumulation had taken place within the historical period, and that Mons Circeius (see on 169 above) was in the Homeric times the Island of Circe in the midst of the open sea.

The Pomptine Marshes are formed principally by the stagnation of the waters of two streams, the Amasenus and the Ufens (see on 177 above), and appear to have derived their name from the city of *Suessa Pometia*, the capital of the Volscians, situated on their border. Various attempts were made to drain these marshes, and a project of this kind was among the great public works planned by Julius Cæsar. The Appian Way was carried through them as early as 312 B.C.

267–272. *The braying of the war-horns*, etc. Note the alliteration and onomatopœia in these lines.

275. *Corselet.* A piece of body armor. The word (also spelled *corslet*) is derived from the old French *cors*, a body, +*el*+*et*, diminutive terminations.

278. *Digentian rock.* The Digentia (now the *Licenza*) was a small river in the country of the Sabines, flowing into the Anio nine miles above Tibur. Cf. Horace, *Epistles*, i. 18. 104 : "gelidus Digentia rivus." Just above its junction with the Anio stands a rocky, projecting hill, which is probably the *rock* here referred to.

280. *Bandusia's flock.* As indicated here, the Fount of Bandusia, celebrated by Horace in a beautiful ode (iii. 13), has been supposed to be situated near his Sabine villa, and to be the fount alluded to in *Epistles*, I. 16. 12 fol. ; but it seems to have been conclusively proved that the real *fons Bandusiae* was in Apulia, a few miles from Venusia, the birthplace of Horace.

281. *Herminius.* See on *Horatius*, 245 above.

283. *Auster* (the South Wind, or the hot, burning wind, as the derivation implies) is an appropriate name for a swift and fiery steed.

288. *Fidenæ.* A city on the left bank of the Tiber, on the *Via Salaria*, five miles from Rome. It was originally and properly a Latin city, although Livy alludes to it as Etruscan, and even says that its inhabitants learned Latin only from their intercourse with the Roman colonists. It early engaged in wars with Rome, and was captured by Tarquinius Priscus. It was finally subdued by the Romans, and vanishes from history as an independent city in 426 B.C.

294. *Calabrian brake.* Calabria was the name given by the Romans to the peninsula forming the *heel* of Italy, which was called by the Greeks *Messapia* and *Iapygia*. During the time of the Byzantine emperors, the name of Calabria was transferred to the Bruttian peninsula (of which it is to-day the designation), probably because the term at first denoted all the Byzantine possessions in southern Italy, which gradually contracted to the Bruttian peninsula and a very small tract in the Iapygian promontory.

Brake = bush, thicket. "The idea is of rough *broken* ground with the growth which springs from it."

295. *When through the reeds*, etc. Cf. Virgil, *Æneid*, ii. 379 fol. (imitated from Homer, *Iliad*, iii. 33) :

> " Improvisum aspris veluti qui sentibus anguem
> Pressit humi nitens, trepidusque repente refugit
> Attollentem iras et caerula colla tumentem ;
> Haud secus Androgeos visu tremefactus abibat.''

303. *Tubero.* A common Latin name.

308. *Among his elms.* On which trees the grape-vine was trained.
See Virgil, *Ecl.* ii. 70: " Semiputata tibi frondosa vitis in ulmo est ;"
Catullus, 62. 54: " (Vitis) coniuncta ulmo marito ;" and Juvenal, 6. 150:
" ulmi Falernae '' (Falernian *elms* for Falernian *wine*).

325. *Clients.* Supposed to be from the same root as *cluere*, to hear or
obey. Any foreigner or Roman citizen who wanted a protector might
attach himself to a *patronus* and so become a *cliens*. The patron guarded
the client's interest, both public and private ; the client assisted his patron
with money and with military service. The connection was hereditary,
and the client bore his patron's gentile (family) name.

326. *Bare.* An old form of *bore.*

327. *Helm.* Poetical for *helmet.* Cf. Scott, *Marmion*, vi. 30 :

> " When with the baron's casque the maid
>   To the nigh streamlet ran :
>   *   *   *   *   *   *
>   She filled the helm, and back she hied,'' etc.

348. *And hath bestrode his sire.* That is, stood over him to defend him.
Cf. *Coriolanus*, ii. 2. 96 :

> " He bestrid
> An o'er-press'd Roman, and i' the consul's view
> Slew three opposers.''

353. *Cæso.* Or *Kæso*, a prænomen of the *Fabia gens.*

356. *The brave Fabian race.* The Fabian race was one of the most
ancient patrician families at Rome, tracing its origin to Hercules and
Evander. There were many distinguished members of this family ;
whence Anchises in his enumeration of the heroes of Rome (Virgil,
Æneid, vi. 845) says : " Quo fessum rapitis, Fabii ?"—" alluding to the
numbers and exploits of the Fabii, which tire the narrator who tries to
count them '' (Conington, *ad loc.*). The family was celebrated in early
Roman history. Being looked on with disfavor by their own order, they
offered to carry on the war against Veii at their own cost and alone.
When the offer was joyfully accepted, 306 Fabii marched forth under
the lead of Kæso Fabius to the banks of the Cremera, where they erected
a fortress. After carrying on the war successfully for a time, they were
enticed into an ambuscade, and the whole race perished except one boy,
who had been left at Rome on account of his youth. The story is full of
improbabilities and doubtless mythical.

Another distinguished member of the family was Quintus Fabius Maximus Cunctator, the opponent of Hannibal, of whom Ennius wrote:
" Unus homo nobis cunctando restituit rem," a line which Virgil gives
almost verbally in *Æneid*, vi. 846.

357. *Rex.* The name ot several distinguished Romans, the earliest of whom was tribune 196 B.C.

358. *The priest of Juno's shrine.* Juno was the tutelary divinity of Gabii. See Virgil, *Æneid*, vii. 682 : "quique arva Gabinae Iunonis . . . colunt."

360. *Rome's great Julian line.* The *Julian gens* was one of the most ancient patrician families at Rome, some of its members having attained the highest dignities of the state in the earliest times of the republic. It was doubtless of Alban origin, and is mentioned as one of the Alban families transferred to Rome by Tullus Hostilius and enrolled among the *patres.* Virgil (*Æneid*, i. 267) asserts that Iulus, the mythical ancestor of the race, was the same as Ascanius, and Cæsar claimed the same origin for his family by giving " Venus genetrix " as the word to his soldiers at Pharsalia and Munda.

362. *The Velian hill.* One of the seven hills of Rome, between the Palatine, the Esquiline, and the eastern side of the Forum.

375, 376. *The good house That loves the people well.* The surname of Valerius was *Publicola*, or the people's friend, from the following circumstance : Becoming sole consul by the death of his colleague Brutus, he began to build a house on the Velian hill on the site of the palace of Tarquinius Superbus. Being accused of aiming at regal power, he tore the house down. The Valerian gens enjoyed extraordinary honors and privileges at Rome. Their house on the Velia was the only one in Rome of which the doors were allowed to open outward into the street. In the circus a conspicuous place was set apart for them, where a small throne was erected, an unexampled honor. They were also allowed to bury their dead within the city walls.

383. *Yeomen.* Here apparently = common soldiers (as in Shakespeare, *Rich. III.* v. 3. 338 : "Fight, gentlemen of England! Fight good yeomen ") ; or perhaps men of his body-guard, like the "yeomen of the guard" in the service of the English sovereign.

399. *Play the men.* Show yourselves men. Cf. Shakespeare, *Tempest*, i. 1. 11 : "Play the men."

403. *Like the roar of a burning forest*, etc. Cf. Virgil, *Æneid*, ii. 304 fol. :

> "In segetem veluti cum flamma furentibus austris
> Incidit, aut rapidus montano flumine torrens
> Sternit agros, sternit sata laeta boumque labores,
> Praecipitisque trahit silvas, stupet inscius alti
> Accipiens sonitum saxi de vertice pastor."

408. *Wist.* Knew ; past tense of the old verb, *wit* (A. S. *witan*). Cf. *Exod.* ii. 4 and *Mark* ix. 6.

416. *A Consular of Rome.* That is, a *vir consularis*, one who has been consul, a man of consular rank.

419. *Cossus.* The name of a patrician family of the Cornelian race, which produced many illustrious men in the fifth century B.C., but afterwards sank into oblivion.

439. *Ride as the wolves*, etc. As *if* the wolves, etc. This use of *as* is common in Elizabethan English. Cf. *Macbeth*, i. 4. 11 :

> "To throw away the dearest thing he owed,
>   As 'twere a careless trifle," etc.

441. *Our southward battle.* That is, the portion of our army in that direction. Cf. *Macbeth*, v. 6. 4:

> "You, worthy uncle,
> Shall, with my cousin, your right-noble son,
> Lead our first battle;"

that is, the van of our forces. Cf. 463 and 641 below.

480. *Aufidus.* The principal river of Apulia, and one of the largest in Italy, flowing into the Adriatic. Horace, whose birthplace, Venusia, was only ten miles from the Aufidus—whence he calls himself "longe sonantem natus ad Aufidum" (*Odes*, iv. 9. 2)—alludes repeatedly to the violent and impetuous character of the river, when swollen by winter floods or by heavy rains. In the summer, however, it is an insignificant stream.

Po. The principal river of northern Italy, and by far the largest in the peninsula. Hence *from Aufidus to Po* = from one end of Italy to the other. The *Padus*, or *Po*, was identified by the Greeks with the mythical *Eridanus*, and it was commonly called by that name both by them and by the Roman poets.

495. *Lay on.* Deal blows, strike. Cf. *Macbeth*, v. 8. 33: "Lay on, Macduff;" and *Henry V.* v. 2. 147: "I could lay on like a butcher," etc.

547. *Herminia.* While the Roman man usually had three names, the *prænomen*, the *nomen* proper or *nomen gentilicium*, and a *cognomen*, the Roman women were designated only by the feminine form of the *nomen gentilicium*, having no *prænomen* other than *Prima*, *Secunda*, *Tertia*, etc.

549. *Ribbo..s.* The spelling *ribands* or *ribbands* (in the English eds.) arose from a fancied connection with *band;* but the *d* is "excrescent," as in *hind* (see on *Horatius*, 337 above), and is not always found in Middle English. The word is of Celtic origin, from *ribe*, a flake, hair. The *an* is the common Celtic diminutive termination.

557. *The furies of thy brother.* The *Eumenides* or *Erinnyes*, who, as the Greeks believed, pursued and tormented criminals, especially murderers. Cf. Virgil, *Æneid*, iii. 331: "scelerum Furiis agitatus;" referring to Orestes, who had slain his mother Clytemnestra.

568. *Capuan's hall.* Capua was the capital of Campania (see on *Horatius*, 337 above) and one of the most celebrated and important cities of Italy. The name, like *Campania*, is probably derived from *campus*, from its situation in a fertile plain. Capua was proverbial for luxury and magnificence; the effect on Hannibal's troops of their winter there is much dwelt on by Roman writers. Cf. *Virginia*, 267, 328.

569, 570. *The knees of all the Latines Were loosened with dismay.* An Homeric expression. See *Iliad*, v. 176: ἐπεὶ πολλῶν τε καὶ ἐσθλῶν γού-νατ᾽ ἔλυσεν.

603. *Samothracia.* An island in the north of the Ægæan Sea, opposite the mouth of the Hebrus. Homer calls it sometimes Σάμος Θρηικίη and sometimes simply Σάμος. Hence the line in Virgil, *Æneid*, vii. 208: "Threiciamque Samum, quæ nunc Samothracia fertur." It measures

eight miles by six, and is of great elevation, being the most conspicuous object in the north of the Ægæan except Mt. Athos, and surpassing all the islands but Crete in height. The common name of the Thracian and Ionian Samos was a cause of speculation to Pausanias and Strabo. The truth seems to be that σάμος denoted any elevated land near the sea, and that the name was therefore given to several islands. The chief interest of the island is connected with the mysterious rites of the *Cabeiri* celebrated there, into which Philip of Macedon was initiated with Olympias, his wife. Very little is known about the *Cabeiri*, but by some writers they are identified with the Dioscuri, which is the occasion of the reference here to Samothracia. See *Addenda*, p. 195 below.

604. *Cyrene.* The chief city of the district of Cyrenaica on the north coast of Africa between Carthage and Egypt, and the most important Hellenic colony in Africa. At the height of its power Cyrene had an extensive commerce with Greece and Egypt, especially in *silphium*, a plant with a very strong flavor, the juice of which was used in food and medicine. Cyrene holds a distinguished place in the history of Greek intellect. It was the birthplace of the poet Callimachus, and as early as the time of Herodotus was celebrated for its physicians. As it was an Hellenic colony the worship of the Dioscuri would be observed there, as well as at Tarentum and Syracuse.

605. *Our house in gay Tarentum. House* is here used in the sense of *temple.*

Tarentum was one of the most powerful and celebrated cities of southern Italy, situated in Calabria on the north shore of the extensive Gulf of Tarentum (*Golfo di Taranto*). It was a Greek city, a colony of Lacedæmon, and retained, Polybius tells us, many traces of its Spartan origin in local names and customs. Hence the worship of the Dioscuri probably flourished there. Although its territory was not especially fertile, it was admirably suited for the growth of olives, and its pastures produced wool of the finest quality, while its harbor abounded in all sorts of shell-fish, among them the *murex*, which furnished the celebrated purple dye. Tarentum, however, owed its rapid rise to the excellence of its port, through which it became the chief emporium of the commerce of southern Italy. No traces of the ancient city remain.

The advantages of Tarentum are extolled by Horace in a well-known ode (ii. 6):

> " Unde si Parcae prohibent iniquae,
>   Dulce pellitis ovibus Galaesi
>   Flumen et regnata petam Laconi
>   Rura Phalantho.
>   Ille terrarum mihi praeter omnes
>   Angulus ridet, ubi non Hymetto
>   Mella decedunt viridique certat
>   Baca Venafro :
>   Ver ubi longum tepidasque praebet
>   Iuppiter brumas, et amicus Aulon
>   Fertili Baccho minimum Falernis
>   Invidet uvis.''

607. *Masts of Syracuse.* Syracuse was the most important and powerful of all the Greek cities in Sicily. It had an excellent port called the

Great Harbor, a bay five miles in circumference; and also the Lesser Port between the island of Ortygia and the mainland. It was a Corinthian colony and became very powerful. It is known in history especially on account of the great siege by the Athenians in 414 B.C. during the Peloponnesian war, and its capture by Marcellus in 212 B.C. For a description of its topography see Cicero *in Verrem*, iv. 52, 53.

609. *The proud Eurotas.* The principal river of Laconia, flowing through the whole length of the valley between the ranges of Taÿgetus and Parnon. Its more ancient names were *Bomycas* and *Himerus.* The scenery in the upper part of its course is beautiful; in the lower part, after passing through a gorge twelve miles in length, it flows amid marshes and sandbanks into the Laconian Gulf.

The Dioscuri, who were believed to have reigned as kings of Sparta, received divine honors in that city; thence their worship spread over Greece, Sicily, and Italy.

614. *And each couched low his spear.* That is, levelled the spear, or held it in the proper position. Cf. Shakespeare, 1 *Hen. VI.* iii. 1. 179: "A braver soldier never couched lance."

619. *Ardea.* A city still bearing the same name, about four miles from the sea-coast and twenty-four south of Rome. Its foundation was as-

ARDEA.

signed by some to the son of Odysseus and Circe, by others to Danaë, the mother of Perseus. It was the capital of the Rutuli, with whom Æneas fought. In the historical period Ardea had become a purely Latin city, and was one of the thirty which formed the Latin League. It was besieged by Tarquin the Proud, and it was during this long siege that the events which led to the expulsion of the kings took place. In the legendary history of Camillus Ardea plays an important part, but soon after vanishes from history as an independent city. See Virgil, *Æneid*, vii. 411 :

> " Locus Ardea quondam
> Dictus avis ; et nunc magnum tenet Ardea nomen."

The city was desolate in the time of Virgil.

620. *Cora.* See on 183 above.

623. *The hearth of Vesta.* See on *Horatius*, 229 above.

624. *The Golden Shield.* See on *Horatius*, 81 above. The reference here is to the original *ancile*.

641. *Battle.* See on 441 above.

646. *The Celtic plain.* The Gallic plain.

648. *The Adrian main.* See on 27 above.

649. *Our sire Quirinus. Quirinus* is said by Dionysius of Halicarnassus to be a Sabine word derived from *quiris*, a spear or lance. It was the name given to Romulus after he had been deified, and the festival celebrated in his honor was called the *Quirinalia*. See Virgil, *Æneid*, i. 292 : " Remo cum fratre Quirinus."

656. *The whirling Po.* Professor Wilson, in *Blackwood* (see on *Horatius*, 482 above), after quoting lines 577–656, remarks : "That is the way of doing business. A cut-and-thrust style, without any flourish—Scott's style, when his soul was up, and the first words came like a vanguard impatient for battle."

660. *Lanuvium.* An important city of Latium, on a lofty height, forming a projecting spur or promontory of the Alban Hills towards the south. It was twenty miles from Rome on the right of the Appian Way, a little more than a mile from the road. The name is often written in inscriptions *Lanivium*, and hence was confounded in MSS. with *Lavinium*. It was one of the cities of the Latin League. There was a celebrated temple of Juno Sospita at Lanuvium. Her peculiar garb and attributes are described by Cicero (*De Nat. Deor.* i. 29) and appear on many Roman coins. She was represented with a goat's skin drawn over her head like a helmet, a small shield in her left hand, and peculiar shoes with points turned up (*calceoli repandi*). She was associated on coins with a serpent, and Propertius (iv. 8) tells us that she had a kind of oracle in a sacred grove where a serpent was fed with fruits and cakes by virgins. Pliny (xxxv. 3–6) says that the place was adorned with very ancient but excellent paintings of Helen and Atalanta, which the emperor Caligula in vain attempted to remove.

661. *Nomentum.* A city on the Sabine frontier about four miles from the Tiber and fourteen from Rome. It was really a Latin town, though often considered Sabine. Virgil mentions it among the colonies of Alba (*Æneid*, vi. 773), and its name occurs among the cities of the *Prisci La-*

tini reduced by Tarquinius Priscus. It was undoubtedly a city of the League. It became a country resort for people of quiet tastes. Seneca had a villa there, as well as Nepos and Martial. The latter contrasts its quiet with the splendor and luxury of Baiae.

673. *Arpinum.* A celebrated city of the Volscians, situated on a hill rising above the valley of the Liris. It was the birthplace of Marius and Cicero ; the former was of ignoble birth, but the family of Cicero was one of the most ancient and important at Arpinum, and his father was of the equestrian order. Cicero applies to Arpinum the well-known lines of the *Odyssey* (ix. 27) on Ithaca : τρηχεῖ᾽, ἀλλ᾽ ἀγαθὴ κουροτρόφος, etc. The ancient walls of Arpinum, built in the Cyclopean style, are

GATE OF ARPINUM.

very striking. There is also a gate of singular construction, which is compared with those of Tiryns and Mycenæ.

675. *Metius.* Or *Mettius* ; an old Italian name, in use among the Latins and Sabines.

676. *Anxur.* The Volscian name of the city known to the Romans and Latins as *Tarracina* (now *Terracina*). It was on the Tyrrhenian Sea, about ten miles from Circeii and at the extremity of the Pomptine Marshes. The name *Anxur* is often used for metrical reasons by the Roman poets. See Horace, *Satires*, i. 5. 26 : "Impositum saxis late candentibus Anxur ;" but all prose writers call it Tarracina. It was one of the customary halting-places on the Appian Way, and hence is mentioned by Horace on his journey to Brundisium, in the passage quoted above. The emperor Domitian had a villa there, and Galba was born near by. There were mineral springs in the neighborhood, which seem to have been much frequented. There was a celebrated temple here to Jupiter Anxurus, who was represented as a beautiful youth.

677. *Vulso.* The name of a distinguished patrician family of the *Manlia gens.*

678. *Arician.* See on 172 above.

695. *The Twelve.* The Salii. See on *Horatius*, 81 above.

697. *The High Pontiff.* The *Pontifex Maximus*. Various explanations of the derivation of the word *pontifex* are given. It is probably derived from *pons* and *facere*, but the original meaning is obscure. Some believe that it means the priests who offer sacrifice on the bridge, referring to that of the *Argei* on the sacred Sublician Bridge (see on *Horatius*, 151 above). The *Argei* were certain figures thrown into the Tiber annually from this bridge on the ides of May. The images were twenty-three in number, made of bulrushes, and in the form of men. They took the place of the earlier human sacrifices. The pontifex maximus was the chief of the

TERRACINA.

Roman college of pontiffs, the most illustrious of the great colleges of priests. The institution of the pontiffs was ascribed to Numa, and they were originally five in number, including the pontifex maximus. In 300 B.C. the number was raised to nine, and later to fifteen by Sulla and to sixteen by Julius Cæsar. The college of pontiffs had the superintendence of all matters of religion, private as well as public. They determined in what manner the gods should be worshipped, the proper form of burial, how the *manes*, or spirits of the dead, were to be propitiated, and what signs were to be attended to. The chief pontiff was obliged to live in a *domus publica*. He was chosen from among the most distinguished men in the state, such as had held a curule office or were already members of the college. He appointed the Vestal virgins and the flamens. Originally he was not allowed to leave the city, but in later times this rule was not observed; Cæsar while conquering Gaul was pontifex maximus. In later times the luxurious living of the pontiffs became proverbial. See Horace, *Odes*, ii. 14. 26:

> "mero
> Tinget pavimentum superbo
> Pontificum potiore cenis."

699. *In all Etruria's colleges.* The Etruscans were the instructors of the Romans in many of their religious rites, and the Romans adopted from them a great part of what was in later ages considered the estab-

lished national religion.   The Etruscan religion was especially noted for
its attention to divination.

705. *Young lads*, etc.   Cf. *Horatius*, 58 fol.

716. *Pricking.*   Spurring, riding.   Cf. Spenser, *F. Q.* i. 1. 1: "A gentle knight was pricking o'er the plain."

721. *The great Asylum.*   In order to increase the population of Rome,
Romulus is said to have opened an asylum on the Capitoline hill.   It
was a place of refuge for the inhabitants of other states, rather than for
those who had violated the laws of the city.   See also on *Capys*, 266.

745. *To Vesta.*   See on 7 above.

747. *The well*, etc.   The *Pool* or *Lake of Juturna* between the temples of Vesta and of Castor.   The remains of a low round construction
still to be seen at this point have been supposed to belong to the stone
rim encircling the pool in later times, but this is very doubtful.

760. *The Dorians.*   Here the inhabitants of Lacedæmon.   The Dorians originally dwelt in Doris, a small mountainous district in Central
Greece, between Ætolia and Phocis.   But in the historical period the
whole of the eastern and southern parts of the Peloponnesus was in their
possession.   Their conquest of this region was called the *Return of the
Heraclidæ*, and occurred in prehistoric times.

767, 768. *If once the Great Twin Brethren Sit shining on the sails.*   The
allusion is to the electrical phenomenon called *St. Elmo's fire*, which often
appears on the yards or mastheads of vessels before or during thunder-
storms.   St. Elmo is St. Erasmus of Formia, who is believed by the
mariners of the Mediterranean to have power over tempests, like the
Dioscuri of old.   Some commentators see an allusion to this St. Elmo's
fire in the "lucida sidera" of Horace, *Odes*, i. 3. 2; but the reference
there is probably to the stars Castor and Pollux in the constellation
Gemini.   Cf. Longfellow, *Golden Legend*, v.:

> "Last night I saw Saint Elmo's stars
> With their glimmering lanterns, all at play
> On the tops of the masts and the tips of the spars,
> And I knew we should have foul weather to-day."

774. *A stately dome.*   The temple of Castor and Pollux.   See on 7 above.

780. *Marked evermore with white.*   See on 20 above.

788. *Mars without the wall.*   See on 8 above.

VIRGINIA.

Macaulay's introduction to the poem is as follows:

"A collection consisting exclusively of war-songs would give an imperfect, or rather an erroneous, notion of the spirit of the old Latin ballads.
The patricians, during more than a century after the expulsion of the
kings, held all the high military commands.   A plebeian, even though,
like Lucius Siccius, he were distinguished by his valor and knowledge of
war, could serve only in subordinate posts.   A minstrel, therefore, who

wished to celebrate the early triumphs of his country could hardly take any but patricians for his heroes. The warriors who are mentioned in the two preceding lays—Horatius, Lartius, Herminius, Aulus Posthumius, Æbutius Elva, Sempronius Atratinus, Valerius Poplicola—were all members of the dominant order ; and a poet who was singing their praises, whatever his own political opinions might be, would naturally abstain from insulting the class to which they belonged, and from reflecting on the system which had placed such men at the head of the legions of the commonwealth.

" But there was a class of compositions in which the great families were by no means so courteously treated. No parts of early Roman history are richer with poetical coloring than those which relate to the long contest between the privileged houses and the commonalty. The population of Rome was, from a very early period, divided into hereditary castes, which, indeed, readily united to repel foreign enemies, but which regarded each other, during many years, with bitter animosity. Between those castes there was a barrier hardly less strong than that which, at Venice, parted the members of the Great Council from their countrymen. In some respects, indeed, the line which separated an Icilius or a Duilius from a Posthumius or a Fabius was even more deeply marked than that which separated the rower of a gondola from a Contarini or a Morosini. At Venice the distinction was merely civil. At Rome it was both civil and religious. Among the grievances under which the plebeians suffered, three were felt as peculiarly severe. They were excluded from the highest magistracies ; they were excluded from all share in the public lands ; and they were ground down to the dust by partial and barbarous legislation touching pecuniary contracts. The ruling class in Rome was a moneyed class ; and it made and administered the laws with a view solely to its own interest. Thus the relation between lender and borrower was mixed up with the relation between sovereign and subject. The great men held a large portion of the community in dependence by means of advances at enormous usury. The law of debt, framed by creditors and for the protection of creditors, was the most horrible that has ever been known among men. The liberty and even the life of the insolvent were at the mercy of the patrician money-lenders. Children often became slaves in consequence of the misfortunes of their parents. The debtor was imprisoned, not in a public jail under the care of impartial public functionaries, but in a private workhouse belonging to the creditor. Frightful stories were told respecting these dungeons. It was said that torture and brutal violation were common ; that tight stocks, heavy chains, scanty measures of food, were used to punish wretches guilty of nothing but poverty ; and that brave soldiers whose breasts were covered with honorable scars were often marked still more deeply on the back by the scourges of high-born usurers.

" The plebeians were, however, not wholly without constitutional rights. From an early period they had been admitted to some share of political power. They were enrolled each in his century, and were allowed a share, considerable, though not proportioned to their numerical strength, in the disposal of those high dignities from which they were themselves excluded. Thus their position bore some resemblance to that of the Irish Catholics during the interval between the year 1792 and the year 1829. The plebeians had also the privilege of annually appointing officers named tribunes, who had no active share in the government of the commonwealth, but who, by degrees, acquired a power formidable even to the ablest and most resolute consuls and dictators. The person of the tribune was inviolable; and, though he could directly effect little, he could obstruct everything.

"During more than a century after the institution of the tribuneship, the Commons struggled manfully for the removal of the grievances under which they labored; and, in spite of many checks and reverses, succeeded in wringing concession after concession from the stubborn aristocracy. At length, in the year of the city 378, both parties mustered their whole strength for their last and most desperate conflict. The popular and active tribune Caius Licinius proposed the three memorable laws which are called by his name, and which were intended to redress the three great evils of which the plebeians complained. He was supported, with eminent ability and firmness, by his colleague, Lucius Sextius. The struggle appears to have been the fiercest that ever in any community terminated without an appeal to arms. If such a contest had raged in any Greek city, the streets would have run with blood. But, even in the paroxysms of faction, the Roman retained his gravity, his respect for law, and his tenderness for the lives of his fellow-citizens. Year after year Licinius and Sextius were re-elected tribunes. Year after year, if the narrative which has come down to us is to be trusted, they continued to exert, to the full extent, their power of stopping the whole machine of government. No curule magistrate could be chosen; no military muster could be held. We know too little of the state of Rome in those days to be able to conjecture how, during that long anarchy, the peace was kept, and ordinary justice administered between man and man. The animosity of both parties rose to the greatest height. The excitement, we may well suppose, would have been peculiarly intense at the annual election of tribunes. On such occasions there can be little doubt that the great families did all that could be done, by threats and caresses, to break the union of the plebeians. That union, however, proved indissoluble. At length the good cause triumphed. The Licinian laws were carried. Lucius Sextius was the first plebeian consul, Caius Licinius the third.

"The results of this great change were singularly happy and glorious. Two centuries of prosperity, harmony, and victory followed the reconciliation of the orders. Men who remembered Rome engaged in waging petty wars almost within sight of the Capitol lived to see her the mistress of Italy. While the disabilities of the plebeians continued, she was scarcely able to maintain her ground against the Volscians and Hernicians. When those disabilities were removed, she rapidly became more than a match for Carthage and Macedon.

"During the great Licinian contest the plebeian poets were, doubtless, not silent. Even in modern times songs have been by no means without influence on public affairs; and we may therefore infer that, in a society where printing was unknown and where books were rare, a pathetic or humorous party-ballad must have produced effects such as we can but faintly conceive. It is certain that satirical poems were common at Rome from a very early period. The rustics, who lived at a distance from the seat of government, and took little part in the strife of factions, gave vent to their petty local animosities in coarse Fescennine verse. The lampoons of the city were doubtless of a higher order; and their sting was early felt by the nobility. For in the Twelve Tables, long before the time of the Licinian laws, a severe punishment was denounced against the citizen who should compose or recite verses reflecting on another.* Satire is, indeed, the only sort of composition in which the Latin poets whose works have come down to us were not mere imitators of foreign models; and it is therefore the only sort of composition in which they have never been rivalled. It was not, like their tragedy, their comedy, their epic and lyric poetry, a hot-house plant which, in return for assiduous and skilful culture, gave only scanty and sickly fruits. It was hardy and full of sap; and in all the various juices which it yielded might be distinguished the flavor of the Ausonian soil. 'Satire,' said Quintilian, with just pride, 'is all our own.' Satire sprang, in truth, naturally from the constitution of the Roman government and from the spirit of the Roman people, and, though at length subjected to metrical rules derived from Greece, retained to the last an essentially Roman character. Lucilius was the earliest satirist whose works were held in esteem under the Cæsars. But, many years before Lucilius was born, Nævius had been flung into a dungeon and guarded there with circumstances of unusual rigor, on account of the bitter lines in which he had attacked the great Cæcilian family.† The genius and spirit of the Roman satirists survived the liberty of their country, and were not extinguished by the cruel despotism of the Julian and Flavian emperors. The great poet who told the story of Domitian's turbot was the legitimate successor of those forgotten minstrels whose songs animated the factions of the infant republic.

"Those minstrels, as Niebuhr has remarked, appear to have generally taken the popular side. We can hardly be mistaken in supposing that, at the great crisis of the civil conflict, they employed themselves in versifying all the most powerful and virulent speeches of the tribunes, and in heaping abuse on the leaders of the aristocracy. Every personal defect, every domestic scandal, every tradition dishonorable to a noble house, would be sought out, brought into notice, and exaggerated. The illustrious head of the aristocratical party, Marcus Furius Camillus, might perhaps be, in some measure, protected by his venerable age and by the memory of his great services to the state. But Appius Claudius Crassus enjoyed no such immunity. He was descended from a long line of ancestors distinguished by their haughty demeanor and by the inflexibility with which they had withstood all the demands of the plebeian or-

---

* Cicero justly infers from this law that there had been early Latin poets whose works had been lost before his time. "Quamquam id quidem etiam xii tabulae declarant, condi jam tum solitum esse carmen, quod ne liceret fieri ad alterius injuriam lege sanxerunt" (*Tusc.* iv. 2).

† Plautus, *Miles Gloriosus.* Aulus Gellius, iii. 3.

der.   While the political conduct and the deportment of the Claudian
nobles drew upon them the fiercest public hatred, they were accused of
wanting, if any credit is due to the early history of Rome, a class of qualities which, in a military commonwealth, is sufficient to cover a multitude
of offences.   The chiefs of the family appear to have been eloquent,
versed in civil business, and learned after the fashion of their age ; but
in war they were not distinguished by skill or valor.   Some of them, as
if conscious where their weakness lay, had, when filling the highest magistracies, taken internal administration as their department of public business, and left the military command to their colleagues.*   One of them
had been intrusted with an army, and had failed ignominiously.†   None
of them had been honored with a triumph.   None of them had achieved
any martial exploit, such as those by which Lucius Quinctius Cincinnatus,
Titus Quinctius Capitolinus, Aulus Cornelius Cossus, and, above all, the
great Camillus, had extorted the reluctant esteem of the multitude.   During the Licinian conflict, Appius Claudius Crassus signalized himself by
the ability and severity with which he harangued against the two great
agitators.   He would naturally, therefore, be the favorite mark of the
plebeian satirists ; nor would they have been at a loss to find a point on
which he was open to attack.

"His grandfather, called, like himself, Appius Claudius, had left a name
as much detested as that of Sextus Tarquinius.   This elder Appius had
been consul more than seventy years before the introduction of the Licinian laws.   By availing himself of a singular crisis in public feeling, he
had obtained the consent of the Commons to the abolition of the tribuneship, and had been the chief of that Council of Ten to which the whole
direction of the state had been committed.   In a few months his administration had become universally odious.   It had been swept away by an
irresistible outbreak of popular fury ; and its memory was still held in
abhorrence by the whole city.   The immediate cause of the downfall of
this execrable government was said to have been an attempt made by
Appius Claudius upon the chastity of a beautiful young girl of humble
birth.   The story ran that the Decemvir, unable to succeed by bribes and
solicitations, resorted to an outrageous act of tyranny.   A vile dependant
of the Claudian house laid claim to the damsel as his slave.   The cause
was brought before the tribunal of Appius.   The wicked magistrate, in
defiance of the clearest proofs, gave judgment for the claimant.   But the
girl's father, a brave soldier, saved her from servitude and dishonor by
stabbing her to the heart in the sight of the whole Forum.   That blow
was the signal for a general explosion.   Camp and city rose at once ; the
Ten were pulled down ; the tribuneship was re-established ; and Appius
escaped the hands of the executioner only by a voluntary death.

"It can hardly be doubted that a story so admirably adapted to the
purposes both of the poet and of the demagogue would be eagerly seized
upon by minstrels burning with hatred against the patrician order, against
the Claudian House, and especially against the grandson and namesake
of the infamous Decemvir.

---

* In the years of the city 260, 304, 330.   † In the year of the city 282.

"In order that the reader may judge fairly of these fragments of the Lay of Virginia, he must imagine himself a plebeian who has just voted for the re-election of Sextius and Licinius. All the power of the patricians has been exerted to throw out the two great champions of the Commons. Every Posthumius, Æmilius, and Cornelius has used his influence to the utmost. Debtors have been let out of the workhouses on condition of voting against the men of the people ; clients have been posted to hiss and interrupt the favorite candidates ; Appius Claudius Crassus has spoken with more than his usual eloquence and asperity ; all has been in vain ; Licinius and Sextius have a fifth time carried all the tribes ; work is suspended ; the booths are closed ; the plebeians bear on their shoulders the two champions of liberty through the Forum. Just at this moment it is announced that a popular poet, a zealous adherent of the tribunes, has made a new song which will cut the Claudian nobles to the heart. The crowd gathers round him, and calls on him to recite it. He takes his stand on the spot where, according to tradition, Virginia, more than seventy years ago, was seized by the pander of Appius, and he begins his story."

3. *Tribunes.* See on *Horatius,* 267 above.

10. *Of fountains running wine.* A familiar touch of fancy in ancient legends, as in those of later times.

11. *Of maids with snaky tresses.* Like the Gorgon Medusa, slain by Perseus. Athena afterwards placed her head, which was so terrible that whosoever looked at it was turned to stone, in the centre of her ægis.

12. *Sailors turned to swine.* The allusion is to the transformation of the companions of Odysseus by the enchantress Circe.

20. *The wicked Ten.* The Decemvirs. In 462 B.C. a law was proposed by the tribune C. Terentillus Arsa that a commission should be appointed for drawing up a code of laws. At that time none but the patricians knew the laws, so that they were able to take advantage of the plebeians. The proposition was bitterly opposed by the patricians, and it was only after a struggle of nine years that they consented to send a commission of three men to Greece to collect information about the laws and customs of the Greeks. In 451 B.C. the Decemvirs, all patricians, were appointed. The whole government of the state was put into their hands, all other magistrates, including the tribunes, being obliged to abdicate. Each of the Decemvirs governed one day in turn, and the fasces were carried only before the one in power. During the first year their rule was just and impartial, and, as their work was unfinished at the end of the year, Decemvirs were again chosen, of whom Appius Claudius alone belonged to the former body. These second Decemvirs acted in a most tyrannical fashion. Twelve lictors with the axes and fasces attended each. They made common cause with the patricians, and inflicted all manner of outrages on plebeians. Finally, the act of Appius Claudius here described led to their deposition and the re-establishment of the usual magistrates. The story, like most of the early Roman legends, is full of improbabilities, of which the most glaring is the statement that a commission was sent from Rome to Greece to get material for a code of laws.

27. *Twelve axes.* That is, lictors. See on *Lake Regillus,* 2 above.

30. *Askance.* Obliquely. Cowper (Homer's *Iliad,* xi.) writes "with his eyes askant." The literal sense is "on the slope." It is little else than another form of *aslant.*

32. *Alway.* See on *Horatius,* 68 above.

40. *Client.* See on *Lake Regillus,* 325 above.

45. *Such varlets pimp and jest for hire,* etc. The reference is to the *parasites,* or professional diners-out, who are so admirably delineated in the comedies of Plautus and Terence. They tried to amuse people with their jests, and cheerfully bore all sorts of humiliation and ridicule for the sake of getting a good dinner without paying for it. A specimen of the wit of these buffoons, who in later times existed at Rome as well, is given by Horace in his Journey to Brundisium (*Satires,* i. 5. 52 fol.).

Varlet. The older spelling was *vaslet,* which is for *vassalet,* a diminutive of *vassal.* It meant originally a young vassal, a youth ; hence a servant (*valet*) ; and finally it came to be a term of reproach.

46. *The lying Greeks.* The Romans had a profound contempt for the Greeks, whom they looked on as false and cunning. See Juvenal, iii. 74 :

> " Ede, quid illum
> Esse putes ? quem vis hominem secum attulit ad nos;
> Grammaticus, rhetor, geometres, pictor, aliptes,
> Augur, schoenobates. medicus, magus, omnia novit
> Graeculus esuriens : in caelum, iusseris, ibit.

61. *Her small tablets.* These tablets consisted of two, or sometimes three, thin pieces of wood, of which the outer surfaces were plain, while the inner were covered with wax, surrounded by a narrow rim of wood. They were written on by means of the *stylus,* which was an iron instrument resembling a pencil in size and shape. At one end it was sharpened to a point for writing on the wax, while the other was flat and circular for erasing what had been written.

TABULÆ AND STYLUS.

63. *From the school.* The schools were then kept in booths or stalls around the forum.

69. *The Sacred Street.* The Sacra Via, the most ancient and important street in Rome. It began just east of the Colosseum, passed through the arch of Titus, crossed the Forum, from which, as the *Clivus Capitolinus,* it rose to the depression between the Capitolium and the Arx, whence branches led to the citadel and to the temple of Jupiter.

73. *How for a sport the princes,* etc. When Tarquin was besieging Ardea (see on *Lake Regillus,* 619 above) the king's sons and their cousin Tarquinius Collatinus got into a dispute about the merits of their wives. As nothing was going on at Ardea, they mounted their horses, intending to return to their homes unexpectedly. They first went to Rome,

where they surprised the king's daughters at a splendid banquet. From there they hastened to Collatia where, although it was already late at night, they found Lucretia among her handmaids spinning.

92. *Curled the thin wreaths of smoke.* Wilkins, in his *Primer of Roman Antiquities,* comparing the appearance of a Roman and an English town, says: "The faint blue smoke that curled gently up from the *atrium* furnished a magic veil very different from the dingy pall that broods over English towns."

94. *The Forum.* See on *Lake Regillus,* 7 above.

99. *Panniers.* Strictly bread-baskets (from the Latin *panis,* bread).

128. *Punic.* Carthaginian. Cf. *Capys,* 111, 173.

130. *Brand.* A sword. See on *Horatius,* 189 above.

131. *Flesher.* Butcher; properly a Scottish word.

139. *Cuitiff.* A mean fellow, a wretch; originally merely a captive, from the Latin *captivus,* through the old French *chaitif* (now *chétif*).

147. *The year of the sore sickness.* In the year 463 B.C. a great plague raged at Rome. The consul P. Servilius Priscus, and the augurs M. Valerius and T. Virginius Rutilus died of it. See Livy, iii. 7. According to this, Virginia would be but fourteen years old in 449 when these events took place, but the Roman girls matured young.

150. *The month of wail and fright.* September was always an unhealthy month at Rome, and in later times those who could do so left the city then for country or seaside resorts. See Horace, *Epistles,* i. 16. 16 : "Incolumem tibi me praestant Septembribus horis;" and *Odes,* ii. 14. 15 :

> "Frustra per autumnos nocentem
>   Corporibus metuemus austrum.'

LITUUS.

151. *Augurs.* For the derivation and meaning of the word, see on *Horatius,* 388 above. The college of augurs originally consisted of three members, but the number was afterwards increased to nine. The only distinction in the college was one of age; an elder augur always voted before a younger, even if the latter held one of the higher offices in the state. See Cicero, *De Senectute,* 18. 64: "Multa in nostro collegio praeclara, sed hoc . . . in primis, quod, ut quisque aetate antecedit, ita sententiae principatum tenet, neque solum honore antecedentibus, sed eis etiam, qui cum imperio sunt, maiores natu augures anteponuntur." As insignia of their office they wore the *trabea,* a saffron robe ornamented with horizontal stripes of purple, and carried the *lituus,* a curved wand, which is often represented in various forms on works of art.

177. *That column,* etc. The monument in

the forum known as the *pila Horatia* (or *Horatiana*). It was erected in the reign of Tullus Hostilius, to commemorate the victory of the three Horatii over the Curatii, and bore the spoils taken from the latter. See Livy, i. 26.

187. *Quirites.* Originally the inhabitants of the Sabine town of Cures. After the Sabines and the Romans had united in one community, under Romulus, the name of *Quirites* was taken in addition to *Romani*, the Romans calling themselves in a civil capacity *Quirites*, while in a political and military capacity they retained the name of *Romani*. It was a reproach for soldiers to be called *Quirites*, and Suetonius (*Cæsar*, 70) says that Cæsar once quelled a mutiny by addressing the rebellious soldiers as "Quirites."

189. *Servius.* Servius Tullius, the sixth king of Rome, who, according to the tradition, reformed the Roman constitution, and established the *Comitia Centuriata.* He divided the entire population, plebeians and patricians alike, into five great classes on the basis of wealth. Each of the classes was divided into a certain number of *centuries* or companies, half of which consisted of *seniores* from the age of 46 to 60, and half of *juniores* from 17 to 45. At the head of the classes were the *equites* (see on *Lake Regillus*, 3 above). The five classes formed 192 centuries, including four centuries of smiths, carpenters, and horn-blowers, each century having one vote. Citizens whose property was less than 12,500 *asses* of copper were not included in the classes, and formed a single century. This arrangement, which gave the balance of power to wealth and age, seems to have continued unchanged until after the First Punic War. At some time between the First and Second Punic Wars, a new arrangement was made on the basis of the 35 tribes. The old division into five classes was retained, but for each tribe there were two centuries of each class, which with the 18 centuries of knights, the guilds of horn-blowers, smiths, and carpenters, and a century of those who had no property, made 373 in all.

193. *Did those false sons*, etc. Lucius Junius Brutus, the liberator and first consul of Rome, put to death his two sons, when they were detected with some other young Roman nobles in a conspiracy to restore Tarquin. Cf. Virgil, *Æneid*, vi. 820 foll. :

> "natosque pater nova bella moventes
> Ad poenam pulchra pro libertate vocabit,
> Infelix ! Utcumque ferent ea facta minores,
> Vincet amor patriae laudumque immensa cupido."

195. *Scævola.* When King Porsena was besieging Rome, C. Mucius, a young patrician, went out of the city, telling the senate he was going not for plunder, but for some noble deed. He attempted to assassinate the king, but by mistake killed his secretary, who was dressed very much like the king himself. When seized and brought before Porsena, he boldly declared his design of killing the king himself, and told him that there were many more Roman youths who had sworn to take his life. Porsena ordered him to be burnt alive, unless he would more fully explain his threat, when Mucius thrust his right hand into a fire which was

lighted for a sacrifice, and held it there until it was entirely consumed. The king was so amazed at his firmness that he bade him go away free. Mucius then told him that three hundred of the noblest young men at Rome had sworn to kill the king, and that the lot had first fallen on him. Porsena became alarmed, and made proposals of peace to the Romans. Mucius, on account of the loss of his right hand, received the name of *Scævola*, or *left-handed*. He was given a tract of land across the Tiber called the *Mucia Prata*.

197. *Fox-earth*. The fox's hole ; used here for the animal itself.

204. *The Sacred Hill*. See on *Lake Regillus*, 14 above.

207. *The Marcian fury*. The reference is to Gaius Marcus, surnamed Coriolanus, from his capture of Corioli, who was exiled by the plebeians because he attempted to force them to give up their tribunes, advising the senate, if they refused, not to distribute to them a present of corn which had come from Sicily in a time of famine. He went to Antium and led the Volscians against Rome. He took town after town, and advanced within five miles of the city, ravaging the lands of the plebeians, but sparing those of the patricians. After distinguished embassies had been sent in vain, he yielded to the prayers of a delegation of the noblest matrons headed by his aged mother Veturia and his wife Volumnia.[*] He led the Volscians home again and was put to death by them. See Shakespeare's *Coriolanus*. In addition to the many improbabilities in the story, Livy tells us that Scipio Africanus (201 B.C.) was the first Roman to receive a surname from his conquests. See on *Lake Regillus*, 84 above.

208. *The Fabian Pride*. See on *Lake Regillus*, 356 above.

209. *The fiercest Quinctius*. Cæso, son of L. Quinctius Cincinnatus, the dictator, distinguished himself as a violent opponent of the plebeians. He was a high-spirited young man, distinguished for his strength and size. He and his companions, as Livy tells us (iii. 11), often drove the tribunes from the forum and put the plebeians to flight. He was brought to trial by one of the tribunes, and in spite of his father's efforts was in danger of condemnation through the evidence of one Volscius. He fled from the city, forfeiting his bail, which was mercilessly exacted from his father. Volscius was afterwards arraigned and went into voluntary banishment. Cæso died in exile.

211. *The haughtiest Claudius*. Probably the decemvir's grandfather, who was a bitter enemy of the plebeians.

221. *No crier to the polling*, etc. The people were called together for voting by three distinct acts. The first was a general invitation (*inlicium*) to come to the assembly. While the invitation was being proclaimed, a horn was blown. When upon this signal the people assembled in irregular masses, there followed a second call, when the crowd separated, grouping themselves according to their ages and classes. Hereupon the consul appeared, and led the *exercitus*, as it was called (the arrangement was originally for military purposes), out of the city to the Campus Martius, where the election took place.

---

[*] Plutarch calls his mother Volumnia and his wife Virgilia ; and Shakespeare follows Plutarch in this.

229. *The holy fillets.* The insignia of the priesthoods, to which the patricians alone were eligible. See on *Capys*, 71 below.

230. *The purple gown.* Not entirely of purple, but with a broad purple border; the *toga praetexta*, the badge of senatorial rank. Togas wholly of purple were worn by the Roman emperors; they seem to have been first assumed by Julius Cæsar.

231. *The curule chair.* The *sella curulis*, or chair of state, originally a symbol of kingly power. Cf. 488 and 532 below. Under the republic the right of sitting on this chair belonged to the consuls, prætors, curule ædiles, and censors; also to the dictator and the *magister equitum* (all of which offices were open only to patricians at this time). It was very plain, resembling a common folding camp-stool, but with curved legs. The cut shows a curule chair, and also two pair of bronze legs for such chairs. It has been supposed that the word *curulis* was derived from *curvus*, from the shape of the chair, but it seems to be an adjective from *currus*, a chariot or car.

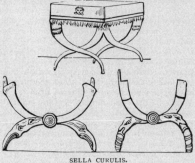

SELLA CURULIS.

232. *The car.* The *quadriga*, or four-horse chariot, in which the Roman generals and emperors rode when they triumphed. *The laurel crown* was also one of the triumphal insignia.

233. *Cohorts.* The cohort was a tenth part of the legion. See on *Capys*, 180 below.

238. *Leech-craft.* Medical skill. See on 367 and 433 below.

239. *Usance.* Interest paid for the use of money, here used as synonymous with *usury.* Cf. Shakespeare, *M. of V.* i. 3. 46: "Brings down the rate of usance here in Venice."

244. *Noisome.* Annoying, offensive. Formed from the

QUADRIGA.

MiddleEnglish *noy*, annoyance, with the suffix *some*, as in *winsome. Noy* is a contraction of *anoy.* It is not connected (as *noise* and *nuisance* are) with the Latin verb *nocere*, but is derived from *in odio* as employed in certain common idiomatic phrases (*in odio habere*, etc.).

246. *In dog-star heat.* The period of most intense heat, which at one time corresponded with the heliacal rising of Sirius, the dog-star, was called in the language of the people *Canis Exortus* long after the two periods of time no longer corresponded ; just as among ourselves the term *dog-days* is used without regard to the actual position of the constellation at the time. The allusions to the dog-star in Latin poetry are numerous. Horace calls it *flagrans,* burning, and *rubra,* red. See also Virgil, *Æneid,* iii. 141 : "tum sterilis exurere Sirius agros."

248. *Holes for free-born feet.* That is, stocks in which the feet were confined.

260. *And ancient Alban kings.* The town of Alba Longa (see on *Capys,* 3 below) was older than Rome. According to the tradition, Ascanius, son of Æneas, founded Alba three hundred years before the founding of Rome by Romulus. See Virgil, *Æneid,* i. 267-277.

265. *In Corinthian mirrors.* The mirrors of the ancients were commonly made of metal, at first of a composition of tin and copper, afterwards usually of silver, but sometimes of gold and precious stones. Silver mirrors are mentioned by Plautus, but the mirrors here referred to are likely to have been of bronze. Corinth was celebrated for its bronze work. The finest bronze known to the Romans was called *aes Corinthiacum,* which was said to have been an alloy made accidentally, in the first instance, by the melting and running together of various metals, especially gold and bronze, at the burning of Corinth by Mummius, 146 B.C.

267. *Capuan odors.* An allusion to the luxury of Capua. Cf. 328 below, and see on *Lake Regillus,* 568 above.

268. *Spanish gold.* The Spanish peninsula abounded in mines of precious metals, which made it attractive to civilized nations from the earliest times.

289-356. *Straightway Virginius led the maid,* etc. Professor Wilson (*Blackwood,* vol. 52, p. 819) remarks : " This is the only passage in the volume that can be called—in the usual sense of the word—pathetic. It is, indeed, the only passage in which Mr. Macaulay has sought to stir up that profound emotion. Has he succeeded ? We hesitate not to say he has, to our heart's desire. Pity and terror are both there—but pity is the stronger ; and, though we almost fear to say it, horror there is none—or, if there be, it subsides wholly towards the close, which is followed by a feeling of peace. This effect has been wrought simply by letting the course of the great natural affections flow on, obedient to the promptings of a sound, manly heart, unimpeded and undiverted by any alien influences, such as are but too apt to steal in upon inferior minds when dealing imaginatively with severe trouble, and to make them forget, in the indulgence of their own self-esteem, what a sacred thing is misery."

291. *Shambles.* Stalls on which butchers expose meat for sale ; hence a slaughter-house. Here the word has its original meaning. It is derived, with an excrescent *b* (as in *number* from *numerus,* etc.), from the Latin *scamellum,* a little bench or stool.

295. *The great sewer.* The famous *Cloaca Maxima,* said to have been made by Tarquinius Priscus to carry off the waters from the valley of the forum to the Tiber. It still serves to some extent its original purpose. It was of great size, the archway where it empties into the Tiber being about twelve feet high. Strabo says that a cart loaded with hay could pass through the *cloaca* in some places. Pliny wondered that it had endured for seven hundred years, but it has now remained for eighteen additional centuries, and seems likely to last as many more.

CLOACA MAXIMA.

298. *Whittle.* Knife. Cf. Shakespeare, *T. of A.* v. 1. 173:

> " There 's not a whittle in the unruly camp
> But I do prize it at my love before
> The reverend'st throat in Athens."

314. *Civic crown.* The *corona civilis* (or *civica*), a wreath of oak leaves, which was given for preserving the life of a citizen in battle and slaying an enemy. The possession of this crown was so high an honor that its attainment was subject to very severe regulations. Before the claim was allowed, it must be proved that the claimant had saved the life of a Roman citizen in battle, slain his opponent, and maintained the ground on which the action took place. The testimony of a third person was not accepted; the person rescued must himself proclaim the fact, which through envy he was often unwilling to do. The soldier who had once won the crown might always wear it; he had a place reserved for him next the senate at all public spectacles; and they, as well as the rest of the company, arose at his entrance. He was freed from all public burdens, as were his father and paternal grandfather. Julius Cæsar won this distinction in his early life, at the siege of Mytilene, 80 B.C. Like other

CORONA CIVICA.

honors, this was voted to Augustus by the senate as the perpetual preserver of the citizens. See Virgil, *Æneid*, vi. 772: "Atque umbrata gerunt civili tempora quercu."

328. *Capua's marble halls.* See on 267 above.

367. *A leech.* A physician; from the A. S. *laéce*, which means the same, and is connected with A. S. *lácnian*, to heal. See Shakespeare, *T. of A.* v. 4. 84:

"make each
Prescribe to other as each other's leech;"

and Spenser, *F. Q.* iii. 4. 43: "For Tryphon of sea gods the soveraine leach is hight."

383. *The judgment-seat.* The tribunal where Appius was sitting.

385. *O dwellers in the nether gloom.* The gods of the lower world and the *manes*, or spirits of the dead. *Nether*=lower; *ther* being a comparative suffix added to *ni*, downward. Cf. Shakespeare, *Lear*, iv. 2. 79: "Our nether crimes" (committed on earth).

409. *The press.* The crowd, throng. Cf. Shakespeare, *J. C.* i. 2. 15: "Who is it in the press that calls on me?"

419. *Porches.* Porticoes, or walks covered with roofs which were supported by columns. They were either attached to temples and other public buildings, or built independent of any other edifice. They were very numerous and extensive about the forum, and were used for the transaction of business and as lounging-places.

426. *With many a cypress crown.* The cypress was the emblem of mourning. A branch of it was placed before the door of a house in which a dead body lay, that no one might enter and be polluted unawares by the presence of death. See also Virgil, *Æneid*, vi. 216: "et feralis ante cupressos Constituunt."

433. *Crafts.* Occupations, business. Originally *craft* meant skill, ability; it is from the A. S. *craeft*, power. Cf. *leech-craft*, 238 above.

437, 438. *The voice of grief and fury*, etc. The reading of the early eds. was:

"Till then the voice of pity
And fury was not loud."

447. *Sheaf of twigs.* That is, the *fasces*.

455. *The Pincian Hill.* Originally called *Collis Hortorum*, on account of the gardens which covered it. Here was the famous villa of Lucullus. The hill got its name of Pincian at a late period of the Empire, when the Pincian family built a magnificent palace upon it. This palace was the residence of Belisarius during his defence of Rome.

456. *The Latin Gate.* This gate originally stood over the Latin road (*Via Latina*), which led to Tusculum (*Frascati*). It is was walled up in 1808.

463. *And breaking-up of benches.* When Tiberius Gracchus was slain by the "mob of gentlemen," his assailants armed themselves in this way. The benches in the present case stood around the tribunal of the decemvir.

487. *Potsherds.* Bits of pottery. A *sherd* is a *shred*, or fragment. It is also spelled *shard*. It means literally "a broken thing," from the A. S. adj. *sceard*, broken. For the uncompounded word, see *Hamlet*, v. 1. 254: "Shards, flints, and pebbles should be thrown on her."

497. *Caius of Corioli.* See on 207 above.

501. *Furius.* M. Furius Camillus, who was said to have forced the Gauls to leave Rome, after their capture of the city in 390 B.C.; and also to have taken Veii from the Etruscans.

513. *A Cossus.* See on *Lake Regillus*, 419 above.

515. *A Fabius.* See on 208 above.

551. *When raves the Adriatic.* The navigation of the Adriatic was

much dreaded, on account of the frequent and sudden storms to which it was subject. Its bad character in this respect is often alluded to by Horace. Cf. *Odes*, iii. 3. 5: "Dux inquieti turbidus Hadriae." See also *Lake Regillus*, 27 and 647 fol. above.

553. *The Calabrian sea-marks.* For Calabria, see on *Lake Regillus*, 294 above. The *sea-marks* are light-houses or beacons. Pliny mentions the light-houses at Ostia and Ravenna, and says there were similar towers at many other places. The name *pharos* was given to them all from the celebrated light-house at the entrance of the port of Alexandria, which was the model for their construction. The *pharos* at Brundisium was like that at Alexandria, an island with a light-house upon it.

555. *The great Thunder-cape.* Acroceraunia, a very rocky promontory in Epirus, extending into the Ionian sea, nearly opposite Brundisium, which rendered navigation very dangerous. Cf. Horace, *Odes*, i. 3. 20: "Infames scopulos Acroceraunia." It is said to have received its name on account of the many thunder-storms which visited it. See Byron, *Childe Harold*, iv. 73:

> "And in Chimari heard the thunder hills of fear,
> Th' Acroceraunian mountains of old name."

564. *And swayed from side to side.* Cf. Virgil, *Æneid*, v. 469: "Iactantemque utroque caput."

THE PROPHECY OF CAPYS.

Macaulay's introduction to the poem is as follows:

"It can hardly be necessary to remind any reader that, according to the popular tradition, Romulus, after he had slain his grand-uncle Amulius, and restored his grandfather Numitor, determined to quit Alba, the hereditary domain of the Sylvian princes, and to found a new city. The gods, it was added, vouchsafed the clearest signs of the favor with which they regarded the enterprise, and of the high destinies reserved for the young colony.

"This event was likely to be a favorite theme of the old Latin minstrels. They would naturally attribute the project of Romulus to some divine intimation of the power and prosperity which it was decreed that his city should attain. They would probably introduce seers foretelling the victories of unborn consuls and dictators, and the last great victory would generally occupy the most conspicuous place in the prediction. There is nothing strange in the supposition that the poet who was employed to celebrate the first great triumph of the Romans over the Greeks might throw his song of exultation into this form.

"The occasion was one likely to excite the strongest feelings of national pride. A great outrage had been followed by a great retribution. Seven years before this time, Lucius Posthumius Megellus, who sprang from one of the noblest houses of Rome, and had been thrice consul, was sent ambassador to Tarentum, with charge to demand reparation for grievous injuries. The Tarentines gave him audience in their theatre, where he addressed them in such Greek as he could command, which, we may well believe, was not exactly such as Cineas would have spoken. An exquisite sense of the ridiculous belonged to the Greek character; and closely connected with this faculty was a strong propensity to flippancy and impertinence. When Posthumius placed an accent wrong, his hearers burst into a laugh. When he remonstrated, they hooted him, and called him barbarian, and at length hissed him off the stage as if he had been a bad actor. As the grave Roman retired, a buffoon who, from his constant drunkenness, was nicknamed the Pint-pot, came up with gestures of the grossest indecency, and bespattered the senatorial gown with filth. Posthumius turned round to the multitude, and held up the gown, as if appealing to the universal law of nations. The sight only increased the insolence of the Tarentines. They clapped their hands, and set up a shout of laughter which shook the theatre. 'Men of Tarentum,' said Posthumius, 'it will take not a little blood to wash this gown.' *

"Rome, in consequence of this insult, declared war against the Tarentines. The Tarentines sought for allies beyond the Ionian Sea. Pyrrhus, King of Epirus, came to their help with a large army; and, for the first time, the two great nations of antiquity were fairly matched against each other.

"The fame of Greece in arms as well as in arts was then at the height. Half a century earlier, the career of Alexander had excited the admiration and terror of all nations from the Ganges to the Pillars of Hercules. Royal houses, founded by Macedonian captains, still reigned at Antioch and Alexandria. That barbarian warriors, led by barbarian chiefs, should win a pitched battle against Greek valor, guided by Greek science, seemed as incredible as it would now seem that the Burmese or the Siamese should, in the open plain, put to flight an equal number of the best Engglish troops. The Tarentines were convinced that their countrymen were irresistible in war; and this conviction had emboldened them to treat with the grossest indignity one whom they regarded as the representative of an inferior race. Of the Greek generals then living, Pyrrhus was indisputably the first. Among the troops who were trained in the Greek discipline his Epirotes ranked high. His expedition to Italy was a turning-point in the history of the world. He found there a people who, far inferior to the Athenians and Corinthians in the fine arts, in the speculative sciences, and in all the refinements of life, were the best soldiers on the face of the earth. Their arms, their gradations of rank, their order of battle, their method of intrenchment, were all of Latin origin, and had all been gradually brought near to perfection, not by the study of foreign models, but by the genius and experience of many generations of great native commanders. The first words which broke from the king, when his practised eye had surveyed the Roman encampment, were full of meaning: 'These barbarians,' he said, 'have nothing barbarous in their military arrangements.' He was at first victorious; for his own talents were superior to those of the captains who were opposed to him; and the Romans were not prepared for the onset of the elephants of the East, which were then for the first time seen in Italy—moving moun-

* Dion. Hal., *De Legationibus.*

tains, with long snakes for hands.* But the victories of the Epirotes
were fiercely disputed, dearly purchased, and altogether unprofitable.
At length, Manius Curius Dentatus, who had in his first consulship
won two triumphs, was again placed at the head of the Roman commonwealth, and sent to encounter the invaders. A great battle was
fought near Beneventum. Pyrrhus was completely defeated. He re-
passed the sea ; and the world learned with amazement that a people had
been discovered who, in fair fighting, were superior to the best troops
that had been drilled on the system of Parmenio and Antigonus.

"The conquerors had a good right to exult in their success ; for their
glory was all their own. They had not learned from their enemy how to
conquer him. It was with their own national arms, and in their own national battle-array, that they had overcome weapons and tactics long believed to be invincible. The pilum and the broadsword had vanquished
the Macedonian spear. The legion had broken the Macedonian phalanx.
Even the elephants, when the surprise produced by their first appearance
was over, could cause no disorder in the steady yet flexible battalions of
Rome.

"It is said by Florus, and may easily be believed, that the triumph far
surpassed in magnificence any that Rome had previously seen. The only
spoils which Papirius Cursor and Fabius Maximus could exhibit were
flocks and herds, wagons of rude structure, and heaps of spears and
helmets. But now, for the first time, the riches of Asia and the arts of
Greece adorned a Roman pageant. Plate, fine stuffs, costly furniture,
rare animals, exquisite paintings and sculptures, formed part of the procession. At the banquet would be assembled a crowd of warriors and
statesmen, among whom Manius Curius Dentatus would take the highest
room. Caius Fabricius Luscinus, then, after two consulships and two
triumphs, Censor of the Commonwealth, would doubtless occupy a place
of honor at the board. In situations less conspicuous probably lay some
of those who were, a few years later, the terror of Carthage—Caius Duilius, the founder of the maritime greatness of his country ; Marcus Atilius
Regulus, who owed to defeat a renown far higher than that which he had
derived from his victories ; and Caius Lutatius Catulus, who, while suffering from a grievous wound, fought the great battle of the Ægates, and
brought the first Punic war to a triumphant close. It is impossible to re-
count the names of these eminent citizens without reflecting that they
were all, without exception, plebeians, and would, but for the ever-mem-
orable struggle maintained by Caius Licinius and Lucius Sextius, have
been doomed to hide in obscurity, or to waste in civil broils the capacity
and energy which prevailed against Pyrrhus and Hamilcar.

"On such a day we may suppose that the patriotic enthusiasm of a Latin
poet would vent itself in reiterated shouts of *Io triumphe*, such as were
uttered by Horace on a far less exciting occasion, and in boasts resembling those which Virgil put into the mouth of Anchises. The superior-
ity of some foreign nations, and especially of the Greeks, in the lazy arts
of peace, would be admitted with disdainful candor ; but pre-eminence in

---

* *Anguimanus* is the old Latin epithet for an elephant (Lucretius, ii. 538, v. 1302).

all the qualities which fit a people to subdue and govern mankind would be claimed for the Romans.

"The following lay belongs to the latest age of Latin ballad-poetry. Nævius and Livius Andronicus were probably among the children whose mothers held them up to see the chariot of Curius go by. The minstrel who sang on that day might possibly have lived to read the first hexameters of Ennius, and to see the first comedies of Plautus. His poem, as might be expected, shows a much wider acquaintance with the geography, manners, and productions of remote nations than would have been found in compositions of the age of Camillus. But he troubles himself little about dates, and, having heard travellers talk with admiration of the Colossus of Rhodes, and of the structures and gardens with which the Macedonian kings of Syria had embellished their residence on the banks of the Orontes, he has never thought of inquiring whether these things existed in the age of Romulus."

Professor Wilson, in *Blackwood* (see on *Horatius*, 482 above), remarks: "Perhaps the *Prophecy of Capys* is the loftiest lay of the four. The child of Mars, and foster-son of the she-wolf, is wonderfully well exhibited throughout in his hereditary qualities; and grandly in the Triumph, where the exultation breaks through that all this gold and silver is subservient to the Roman steel—all the skill and craft of refinement and ingenuity must obey the voice of Roman valor. There are many such things scattered up and down Horace's Odes; but we can scarcely remember any that are more spirited, more racy, or more characteristic than these *Lays;* and perhaps the nobility of the early Roman character is as fondly admired and as fitly appreciated by an English freeman as by a courtier of the reign of Augustus."

1. *King Amulius.* According to the legend, he was the younger son of Procas, King of Alba Longa, and deposed his brother Numitor. He allowed Numitor to live in retirement, but killed his only son and made his daughter Rhea Silvia a vestal virgin. By Mars she became the mother of twins, Romulus and Remus. Amulius ordered the mother and her babes to be drowned. Silvia became a goddess, and Romulus and Remus, who had been set adrift in a cradle, floated into the Tiber. A she-wolf took the children to her den and suckled them until they were discovered by Faustulus, a shepherd, who took the boys home, and gave them to his wife, Acca Laurentia, to bring up. When they grew up they restored Numitor to the throne and killed Amulius.

2. *Of the great Sylvian line.* The line of kings descended from Ascanius. Silvius, the son of Ascanius, is said to have been so called because he was born in the woods. All the succeeding kings of Alba bore the cognomen of *Silvius.* According to Virgil, Silvius was the son of Æneas. See *Æneid*, vi. 763:

> "Silvius, Albanum nomen, tua postuma proles,
> Quem tibi longaevo serum Lavinia coniunx
> Educet silvis regem regumque parentem,
> Unde genus Longa nostrum dominabitur Alba."

3. *Alba Longa.* A city of Latium, on the eastern side of Lake Alba-

nus and the northern slope of the Alban Mount. It was destroyed at a very early period, and most of its history is fabulous or poetical. According to the legends, Alba was founded by Ascanius, the son of Æneas, thirty years after the founding of Lavinium. The names of a series of mythical kings are given, and it may possibly be admitted that a Silvian family was the reigning house at Alba. The city is said to have been destroyed by Tullus Hostilius as a punishment for the treachery of its general, Metius Fufetius.

4. *On the throne of Aventine.* Aventinus was one of the mythical kings of Alba, and grandfather of Amulius. He is said to have reigned thirty-seven years.

5. *Camers.* Two mythical personages in the *Æneid* bear this name.

9. *Alba's lake.* Now called *Lago di Albano;* a remarkable lake at the foot of the Alban Mount, twenty miles from Rome. It is of oval form,

LAKE OF ALBA.

about six miles in circumference, and has no natural outlet, being surrounded on all sides by steep precipitous banks of volcanic tufa, some of which rise to a height of two or three hundred feet above the level of the lake. It is undoubtedly the crater of an extinct volcano. It is 918 feet above the sea-level, and its waters are of great depth. In 379 B.C., according to Livy and Dionysius, the Romans built a tunnel to carry off the superfluous waters of the lake at the time of a great flood. The legend connects the tunnel with the siege of Veii. This remarkable work still continues to serve the purpose for which it was constructed. It is 4½ feet wide and 6½ feet high at its entrance. Its height, however, diminishes rapidly to not over two feet, and it is impossible to penetrate more than 130 feet from the entrance. The entrance from the lake is through a flat archway, constructed of large blocks of peperino, with a kind of court or triangular space enclosed by massive masonry, and with a second archway over the actual opening of the tunnel. The opposite end of the tunnel is at a place called *le Mole* near *Castel Savelli*, about a mile from Albano, where the waters that issue from it form a considerable stream, now known as the *Rivo Albano*, which after fifteen miles joins the Tiber. The whole work is cut with the chisel, and is computed to have required a period of not less than ten years for its completion.

11. *Alba's oaks.* The oaks on the Alban Mount, an isolated group of hills, now called *Monti Albani*, nearly forty miles in circumference. The *Mons Albanus* of the ancients (now *Monte Cavo*) is the highest peak, rising about 3100 feet above the sea-level. On the top of this mountain stood the temple of Jupiter Latiaris (cf. Lucan, *Pharsalia*, i. 198: "Et residens celsa Latiaris Iuppiter Alba"), the religious centre and place of worship of Latium before the Roman domination. Here too triumphs were celebrated by Roman generals who had failed to secure from the senate the honors of a regular triumph at Rome. Five instances of this kind of triumph are recorded, of which the most illustrious was that of Marcellus, after his capture of Syracuse in 212 B.C. The remains of the temple on the summit were destroyed in 1788, when the present convent was built; but the great lava blocks of the *Via Triumphalis* leading up to it, with the marks of chariot-wheels on them, remain entire in some places. Virgil (*Æneid*, xii. 134 fol.) represents Juno as standing on this height to survey the country, just as tourists do nowadays.

20. *A poplar crown.* The poplar was sacred to Hercules. Cf. *Æneid*, v. 134: "Cetera populea velatur fronde juventus."

71. *Holy fillets.* The fillet (*vitta*) was made of red and white wool, which was slightly twisted, drawn into the form of a wreath, and used by the Romans for ornament on solemn and sacred occasions. It was tied to the heads of priests by a white ribbon.

93. *Capys.* One of the kings of Alba bore this name.

94. *The sightless seer.* Another instance of a blind prophet is Teiresias, who plays so prominent a part in the mythical history of Greece, particularly in the story of Œdipus.

95. *He trembled*, etc. The effect of divine inspiration. Cf. Virgil, *Æneid*, vi. 46:

> "Cui talia fanti
> Ante fores subito non voltus, non color unus,
> Non comptae mansere comae; sed pectus anhelum,
> Et rabie fera corda tument; maiorque videri
> Nec mortale sonans, adflata est numine quando
> Iam propiore dei."

See also Shakespeare, *Tempest*, ii. 2. 72: "Thou dost me yet but little hurt; thou wilt anon, I know it by thy trembling: now Prosper works upon thee ;" where Caliban mistakes the boozy shakiness of the sailor for the magic influence of Prospero working on him.

105. *Garner.* A granary, of which word it is a doublet. Both are derived from the Latin *granarium.* See Shakespeare, *Coriolanus,* i. 1. 244 : "Take these rats thither To gnaw their garners."

106. *Our vines clasp many a tree.* See on *Lake Regillus,* 308 above.

110. *The Tartessian mine.* Tartessus was a district in the south of Spain, to the west of the Pillars of Hercules. It is identified with the Tarshish of Scripture, where it is represented as a celebrated emporium, rich in iron, tin, lead, silver, and other commodities. It was destroyed at an early date, probably by Hamilcar, the Carthaginian general. See on *Virginia,* 268 above.

111. *For thee no ship,* etc. This apparently refers to the importation of rich fabrics as *luxuries* (as the context implies), not to commerce in general. The Romans made a commercial treaty with Carthage in the first year of the Republic.

115. *Arabia shall not steep thy locks.* Arabia, as the name itself implies, was rich in aromatic plants. Frankincense and other perfumes were imported thence. The ancients used many fragrant and costly oils for perfuming the hair and skin, though these luxuries did not become common at Rome until towards the end of the republic. Their use was common with Eastern nations. See Virgil, *Æneid,* iv. 215 :

> "Et nunc ille Paris cum semiviro comitatu,
> Maeonia mentum mitra crinemque madentem
> Subnixus, rapto potitur."

116. *Nor Sidon tinge thy gown.* A reference to the celebrated Tyrian purple. Tyre and Sidon were often confounded, as in the *Æneid,* where Dido is called Sidonian, but is said to have come from Tyre.

117. *Myrrh.* A bitter, aromatic gum. The Latin word *myrrha* and the Greek μύρρα, from which we derive the English *myrrh,* come from the Arabian *murr,* bitter.

121. *Lucre.* Gain, profit (Latin *lucrum*).

149. *Pomona.* The Roman divinity of the fruit of trees, hence called *Pomorum Patrona.* Her name is evidently connected with *pomum.* Her worship must originally have been of considerable importance, as a special priest, *flamen Pomonalis,* was appointed to attend to her service.

150. *Liber.* A name frequently applied by the Roman poets to the Greek *Bacchus* or *Dionysus,* who was accordingly regarded as identical with the Roman *Liber.* Cicero, however, correctly distinguishes between Dionysus and Liber, who was worshipped by the early Italians in conjunction with Ceres and Libera. *Liber* and *Libera* were ancient Italian divinities, presiding over the cultivation of the vine and the fertility of the fields. The festival of the *Liberalia* was celebrated annually by the Romans on the 17th of March.

151. *Pales.* A Roman divinity of flocks and shepherds, described by some as a male, by others as a female deity. In spite of some indications to the contrary, Pales was certainly feminine. The name seems to be connected with *Palatinus,* the centre of all the earliest legends of Rome, and Pales himself was with the Romans the embodiment of the same ideas as

Pan among the Greeks. The *Palilia* were celebrated on the anniversary of the foundation of the city, April 21.

153. *Venus.* The goddess of love among the Romans. Previous to her identification with the Greek Aphrodite, she was one of the least important divinities in the religion of the Romans, and it is observed by the Romans themselves that her name was not mentioned in any of the documents relating to the kingly period of Roman history.

155. *Ivory.* Less trite than *silvery* as an epithet, and expressive, though some have found fault with it.

169. *The soft Campanian.* The Campanians were notorious for their luxurious habits. See on *Lake Regillus*, 568 above.

173. *Leave to the sons of Carthage,* etc. Here the reference must be to navigation for merely commercial purposes. See on 111 above.

176. *And scrolls of wordy lore.* The books of the ancients were commonly written on leaves of papyrus, which were joined together so as to form one sheet. When the work was finished, it was rolled on a staff, whence it was called *volumen* (our *volume*), from *volvo*, to roll. *Lore*= learning; and from the same root as that word.

On this whole passage, cf. *Æneid*, vi. 847:

> " Excudent alii spirantia mollius aera,
> Credo equidem, vivos ducent de marmore voltus,
> Orabunt caussas melius, caelique meatus
> Describent radio et surgentia sidera dicent :
> Tu regere imperio populos, Romane, memento ;
> Hae tibi erunt artes, pacisque imponere morem,
> Parcere subiectis et debellare superbos.''

177. *The pilum.* A thick strong javelin carried by the Roman legionary soldiers. Its shaft, often of cornel wood, was four and a half feet long, and the barbed iron head, which was fastened to it with great care, was of the same length, but extended half-way down the shaft, so that the whole length of the weapon was about six feet nine inches. Each soldier carried two *pila*.

178. *The sword.* The Roman sword was short and heavy. It had a blade about two feet long and several inches wide. It was pointed and two-edged, and was thus adapted either for cutting or thrusting. Cf. 221 below.

179. *The mound.* The mound, or *agger*, was used in attacking fortified places. It consisted of earth and turf supported by a wooden framework. It was begun at a distance and built with an easy slope to the height of the wall. After it had been pushed as near the wall as practicable, the intervening space was hastily filled, and the besiegers rushed over it into the town.

180. *The legion's ordered line.* The legion was the unit of the Roman army. It contained infantry, cavalry, and, where military engines were extensively used, artillery also. Originally, as formed by Romulus, the legion contained 3000 infantry (1000 from each of the three tribes) and 300 cavalry. The number of foot-soldiers was gradually increased to about 6000. The legion was divided into ten *cohorts*, and each cohort into three *maniples*. The officers were six *military tribunes* and two *centurions* to each maniple. It consisted at first only of Roman citizens. Marius

was the first to admit all classes of citizens. The number of the cavalry remained unchanged. At first it consisted of *equites equo publico* (see on *Lake Regillus*, 3 above), but in Cæsar's time it was composed entirely of auxiliaries. It was divided into ten *decuriae*, each commanded by a *decurion*. The entire force was commanded by a *praefectus equitum*.

181. *And thine the wheels of triumph.* The *triumph* was a solemn procession in which a victorious general entered the city in a chariot drawn by four horses. He was preceded by the captives and spoils taken in war, and was followed by his troops. After passing in state along the Via Sacra (see on *Virginia*, 69 above) he ascended to the Capitol to offer sacrifice in the temple of Jupiter.

When a decisive battle had been won or a province subdued, the imperator forwarded to the senate a laurel wreathed dispatch. If the news was satisfactory, the senate decreed a public thanksgiving. After the war was over, the general returned to Rome, but did not enter the city. A meeting of the senate was held outside the walls, usually in the temple of Bellona, that he might

ROMAN SOLDIER WITH PILUM.

urge his claim in person. Only a dictator, consul, or prætor could triumph; at least 5000 of the enemy must have been slain in battle; the advantage must have been a positive one, and the loss of the Romans small compared with that of the enemy. Moreover it must have been a legitimate contest against public foes, and not a civil war. There were also other minor conditions which were carefully insisted on.

As the procession ascended the Capitoline hill, some of the hostile chiefs were led aside into the adjoining prison and put to death. The victorious general wore a purple toga richly embroidered (*toga picta*) and a tunic adorned with figures worked in gold (*tunica palmata*), carried in his hand an ivory sceptre with an eagle, the sacred bird of Jupiter, at the top, and wore a chaplet of bay leaves.

186. *Vail.* Lower, abase; contracted from the obsolete *avail* or *avale*, the French *avaler* (from Latin *ad vallem*). Cf. *Hamlet*, i. 2. 70:

> " Do not forever with thy vailed lids
> Seek for thy noble father in the dust;"

Measure for Measure, v. 1. 20:

> " Justice, O royal duke! Vail your regard
> Upon a wronged, I would fain have said, a maid!"

Marmion, iii. 234 :

> " And proudest princes vail their eyes
> Before their meanest slave," etc.

Editors and printers often confound this obsolete *vail* with *veil*, especially when it is used with reference to the eyes.

187. *Capua's curled revellers.* See on *Lake Regillus,* 568 above.

189. *The Lucumoes of Arnus.* That is, the Etruscan nobles. See on *Horatius,* 185 above.

191. *The proud Samnites.* The Samnites were a hardy and brave race of mountaineers, dwelling in central Italy. They came into conflict with the Romans in 343 B.C. and waged three wars with them (343–341, 326–304, 298–290), which ended in their complete defeat, although in the second or great Samnite war they inflicted on the Romans the memorable defeat and humiliation of the Caudine Forks in 321. The struggle of Rome with the Samnites as a nation ended with the third Samnite war, but the Samnites fought with Pyrrhus and the Tarentines against Rome, and with their allies were reduced to complete submission in 272 B.C. During the Second Punic War most of the Samnites declared in favor of Hannibal, and in the Social War (90 B.C.) they took a prominent part. They espoused the cause of the Marian party against Sulla, and the battle at the Colline Gate (82 B.C.), in which they were defeated by Sulla after a desperate struggle, was long remembered as one of the greatest dangers to which Rome had ever been exposed. Sulla put to death 8000 prisoners taken in this battle, and carried fire and sword through Samnium, with the express purpose of extirpating the whole race. We learn from Strabo that more than a century later the province was in a state of the utmost desolation.

195. *His fair-haired armies.* See on *Horatius,* 36 above. The "fair-haired Gauls" were persistent and dangerous enemies of Rome. After their capture of the city in 390 B.C., the tide slowly turned in favor of the Romans. In 296 B.C. the Gauls, Etruscans, Umbrians, and Samnites were defeated by the Romans at Sentinum : and three years before the invasion of Pyrrhus the Etruscans and the Boii were defeated with terrible slaughter at Lake Vadimon in Etruria, and again the year after. For forty-five years after these battles the Romans were unmolested by the Gauls, and were enabled to give their undivided attention to their struggle with Pyrrhus and to the first war with Carthage.

197. *The Greek shall come against thee,* etc. Pyrrhus, King of Epirus. For the causes of the war with Pyrrhus and its result see the Introduction. In *The conqueror of the East,* the reference is to the conquests of Alexander the Great, to whose family Pyrrhus was related.

200. *The huge earth-shaking beast.* The reference is of course to the elephant (see p. 182 above), which the Romans first encountered in their struggle with Pyrrhus. The early victories of Pyrrhus (at Heraclea and Asculum) were largely due to the terror which they inspired in the Romans.

205. *The Epirotes.* The followers of Pyrrhus from Epirus, the region west of Thessaly in Northern Greece. Pyrrhus brought over a well-disciplined force of nearly 30,000 Epirotes. The brunt of the battles of

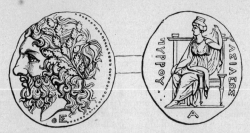

COIN OF PYRRHUS WITH HEAD OF DODONEAN ZEUS.

Heraclea and Asculum, where Pyrrhus lost many men, fell upon them, and their numbers were still further reduced by his expedition to Sicily. Hardly a third of the original force fought in the final battle of Beneventum.

207. *Tarentum.* See on *Lake Regillus*, 605 above.

222. *The thick array*, etc. The reference is to the *Macedonian phalanx*, invented by Philip, father of Alexander the Great, to which the Roman legion showed itself decidedly superior at Cynoscephalæ (197 B.C.), on account of its greater activity.

230. *The Red King.* The Greek word πυρρός, from which the name *Pyrrhus* is derived, means red, or flame-colored.

232. *Is not the gown washed white?* The reference is to the insult offered to the Roman envoy by a drunken Tarentine, for an account of which see p. 181 above.

242. *And goblets rough with gold.* Cf. Virgil, *Æneid*, v. 267 : "Cymbiaque argento perfecta atque aspera signis."

245. *The stone that breathes and struggles*, etc. See quotation from *Æneid* in note on 176 above.

247. *Cunning.* In the old sense of art or skill. Cf. *Psalms*, cxxxvii. 5.

249. *Manius Curius.* M. Curius Dentatus is said to have derived his surname from the circumstance that he was born with teeth. He was a plebeian of Sabine origin, and first distinguished himself when tribune by opposing Appius Claudius Cæcus, who, while presiding at the consular elections, refused to accept any votes for a plebeian candidate. Curius compelled the senate to pass a decree by which any legal election was sanctioned beforehand. In 290 B.C. he and his fellow-consul P. Cornelius Rufinus brought the Samnite war to a close and celebrated a triumph. His second triumph was over the Sabines, who had revolted from Rome. In 275 B.C., when consul for the second time, he defeated Pyrrhus at Beneventum in Samnium, and celebrated his third triumph, the most magnificent that Rome had yet witnessed. It was adorned by four elephants, the first that had been seen at Rome. The next year he was again appointed consul, and defeated the Lucanians, Samnites, and Bruttians. He then retired to private life, and lived with great simplicity on his Sabine farm. In 272 B.C. he was made censor, when he built an

BENEVENTUM IN SAMNIUM.

aqueduct which brought water into the city from the river Anio. He was celebrated down to the latest times as one of the noblest specimens of ancient Roman simplicity and frugality, as well as for the useful works he constructed. At the town of Reate, in the country of the Sabines, he cut a canal from Lake Velinus through the rocks, and thus carried its waters to a place where they fall from a height of 140 feet into the Nar (*Nera*). This fall is still celebrated as that of Terni, or the *Cascade delle Marmore*. See Byron, *Childe Harold*, iv. 69:

> " The roar of waters !—from the headlong height
> Velino cleaves the wave-worn precipice ;
> The fall of waters ! rapid as the light
> The flashing mass foams shaking the abyss," etc.

By this work the inhabitants of Reate obtained a considerable tract of arable land called *Rosea* (cf. 257 below).

254. *The third embroidered gown.* The *toga picta* (see on 181 above) worn in triumphs by the general.

259. *Mevania.* A considerable city of Umbria, on the Flaminian Way. It was situated on the river Tinia in a broad and fertile valley eight or ten miles in width, watered by the Clitumnus and Tinia. It was celebrated for a breed of white oxen, the only ones thought worthy to be sacrificed at triumphs (see on *Horatius*, 46 above). Pliny mentions Mevania as one of the few cities in Italy that had walls of brick. The modern city, *Bevagna*, is a very poor and decayed place with little more than 2000 inhabitants, though retaining its episcopal see and the title of a city. It contains some remains of an amphitheatre and mosaic pavements belonging to the ancient baths.

266. *The Suppliants' Grove.* The *Asylum* of Romulus. See on *Lake Regillus*, 721 above. The exact position of the Asylum is disputed, but

from Livy's words, "Locum, qui nunc septus descendentibus inter duos lucos est, asylum aperuit," it would seem to have been situated under the northeast summit of the Capitoline hill, between the *carcer* and the temple of Concord and behind the arch of Severus. It was near the Asylum that the fire broke out which destroyed the Capitol. See Virgil, *Æneid*, viii. 342:

> "Hinc lucum ingentem, quem Romulus acer Asylum
>   Rettulit."

268. *Capitolian Jove.* The temple of Jupiter, Mars, and Minerva on the Capitoline hill. It was planned by the elder Tarquin, and finished by Tarquinius Superbus. It was 200 feet broad and but fifteen feet longer. Its front had three rows of columns, with two rows on the sides; the back apparently had a plain wall. The interior contained three cells (*cellae*) parallel to one another and with common walls, the one in the centre being Jupiter's. Its name *Capitolium*, according to a well-known legend, was due to the finding of a human head when digging the foundations.

The image of the god was originally of clay. The face was painted vermilion, and the statue was probably clad in the *toga picta* and the *tunica palmata* (see on 181 above). On the *acroterium*, or apex, of the pediment stood a *quadriga* of earthenware, whose portentous swelling in the furnace was regarded as an omen of Rome's future greatness.

After the Capitol was burned in 83 B.C. its restoration was undertaken by Sulla and afterwards confided to Q. Lutatius Catulus. In 69 B.C. it was destroyed by the Vitellians and restored by Vespasian on the original plan, except for a slight increase in height. It was again destroyed, soon after Vespasian's death, in a great fire, and was rebuilt by Domitian with a splendor before unequalled. This building lasted until a late period of the Empire, although nothing further is accurately known of its history.

269. *Where over two bright havens*, etc. *Corinth* was situated on the isthmus connecting Central Greece with the Peloponnesus. Its citadel was a lofty rock called the *Acrocorinthus*. Standing on a narrow isthmus between two important seas at a time when all navigation was performed by coasting vessels, Corinth naturally became a great maritime power and a rich and prosperous city. Horace (*Odes*, i. 7. 2) speaks of "bimaris Corinthi moenia." Cicero (*de Lege Manil.* 5. 11) calls it "totius Graeciae lumen."

When the Achæan League entered into war with Rome, Corinth was its capital, and it was here that the Roman envoys were insulted. The city was taken by L. Mummius in 146 B.C. and was completely destroyed. All the male inhabitants were slain, and the women and children sold into slavery. The most valuable works of art were carried to Rome. Mummius had so little appreciation of their worth as to stipulate with those who transported them that if any were lost he should be replaced by others equally good. Corinth was rebuilt by a colony sent by Julius Cæsar in 46 B.C., and again became a flourishing city.

271. *Where the gigantic King of Day*, etc. *Rhodes* was one of the chief islands of the Ægæan, situated in the Carpathian Sea about ten miles from the coast of Caria. Pliny says that it is 125 Roman miles in cir-

CORINTH.

cumference. All its towns were on the coast. Its name is supposed to be derived from ῥόδον, a rose; and the rose appears as a symbol on the coins of the island. Its situation favored extensive commerce, and during the best period of their history the Rhodians enjoyed great prosperity. According to Strabo, Rhodes surpassed all other cities in the beauty and convenience of its ports, streets, walls, and public edifices, all of which were adorned with many works of art. The bronze statue of Helios here referred to, the famous *Colossus of Rhodes*, was one of the Seven Wonders of the ancient world. It was the work of Chares of Lindos, who spent twelve years in its execution. It cost 300 talents, and was 70 cubits in height; few men were able to compass one of its thumbs with their arms. It was erected at the entrance of one of the ports, but the statement that it stood astride over the entrance, and that the largest ships could sail between its legs, is probably a fable. It was overthrown by an earthquake in 224 B.C., fifty-six years after its erection. The present town of Rhodes contains very few remains of the Greek city.

273. *Orontes.* The most renowned river of Syria. The name is used by Juvenal (iii. 62) for the whole country: "in Tiberim defluxit Orontes." A modern traveller says: "The river is called by the people *El-'Asi*, the rebel, from its *refusal* to water the fields without the compulsion of water-wheels, according to Abulfeda; but more probably from its occasional violence and wanderings during its course of about 200 miles."

276. *Dark-red colonnades.* Built of the red Egyptian granite.

280. *Byrsa.* An ancient name for *Carthage.* According to the story, Dido, the mythical founder of Carthage, purchased from the natives, for an annual tribute, as much land as could be covered with a bull's hide,

but cunningly cut the hide jnto very thin strips and so enclosed a space of 22 stadia. On this she built her city, which afterwards, as the place grew, became the citadel and retained in its name Byrsa (βύρσα, a bull's hide) the memory of the bargain. The legend seems to have been suggested by the name *Byrsa*, which was really a corruption of *Bosra*, the Phœnician name for the citadel of the city. See also on *Lake Regillus*, 203 above. Cf. *Æneid*, i. 367.

283. *Morning-land.* The *Orient*, or East.

285. *Atlas.* The giant who bore the heavens on his shoulders. According to Homer, he knew the depths of all the sea and bore the long columns that kept asunder heaven and earth. The idea of his being a divine being with a personal existence is blended with the idea of a mountain in the Homeric conception. Later myths represent him as a man changed into a mountain. He stood in northwestern Africa near the *Pillars of Hercules*, where the Atlas mountains are situated. Cf. Virgil, *Æneid*, iv. 246:

ATLAS (FARNESE COLLECTION).

"Iamque volans apicem et latera ardua cernit
Atlantis duri, caelum qui vertice fulcit,
Atlantis, cinctum adsidue cui nubibus atris
Piniferum caput et vento pulsatur et imbri ;
Nix umeros infusa tegit ; tum flumina mento
Praecipitant senis, et glacie riget horrida barba."

Professor Wilson (see on *Horatius*, 482 above), in closing his review of the *Lays*, remarks : "It is a great merit of these poems that they are free from ambition or exaggeration. Nothing seems overdone—no tawdry piece of finery disfigures the simplicity of the plan that has been chosen. They seem to have been framed with great artistic skill—with much self-denial and abstinence from anything incongruous—and with a very successful imitation of the effects intended to be represented. Yet every here and there images of beauty and expressions of feeling are thrown out, that are wholly independent of Rome or the Romans, and that appeal to the widest sensibilities of the human heart. In point of homeliness of thought and language, there is often a boldness which none but a man conscious of great powers of writing would have ventured to show."

ADDENDA.

THE TEXT OF THE LAYS.—Macaulay appears to have made very few changes in the text after the *Lays* were published. The only one we feel sure of, besides that noted on *Virginia*, 437, 438, is in *Lake Regillus*, 296, where the early eds. have "painted snake." There are several little variations in the successive eds. which are probably due to the printer. In *Horatius*, 344, nearly all the eds. have "spears' lengths;" but in *Lake Regillus*, 380, all that we have examined read "lances' length." In *Lake Regillus*, 192, 193, the early eds. have "their right" and "Their leader" (cf. 209), while some of the later ones have "the right" and "The leader." In *Capys*, 215, one ed. has "On the fat and on the eyes;" but all the others read as in our text, which is probably what Macaulay wrote. In *Capys*, 266, all the eds. read "Suppliant's Grove;" but, if the reference is to the Asylum of Romulus, this is probably a misprint. We have not met with the Latin equivalent of *Suppliants' Grove* in our reading, and suspect that the name was coined by Macaulay for the sake of the rhyme. In most of the American eds. there are many little misprints.

The Latian name (*Horatius*, 97).—*Nomen Latinum* was the name applied by the Romans to the colonies founded by Rome which did not enjoy the rights of Roman citizenship, and which stood in the same position with regard to the Roman state that had been formerly occupied by the cities of the Latin League. The name originated at a time when colonies were actually sent out in common by the Romans and the Latins; but similar colonies continued to be sent out by the Romans alone long after the extinction of the Latin League.

The Fair Fount (*Lake Regillus*, 43).—If Macaulay, who is generally so accurate in his topography (according to the authorities of his time), did not imply that the *Fair Fount* was somewhere on the battle-field of Lake Regillus, we should suspect that he had in mind the fountain on Horace's Sabine farm, formerly supposed to be the *Fons Bandusiae* (see on 280), and now known as *Fonte Bello*. Some of the American eds. print this line "Upon the Turf by the Fair Fount;" but all the English eds. have "turf."

Nomen gentilicium (note on *Lake Regillus*, 547).—In the dictionaries of antiquities this term is given as a synonym of "the *nomen* proper;" but the word *gentilicium* is found only in late Latin, and rarely even there.

Samothracia (*Lake Regillus*, 603). — The excavation of temples of the *Cabeiri* (or *Kabeiroi*) in Samothrace, and lately near Thebes in Bœotia, shows that they belonged to the Class of *Chthonian* or under-world deities. From the inscriptions found during the Bœotian excavations they appear to have been worshipped as father and son, not as brothers. The inscriptions read "The Kabeiros and his Son."

CARPENTUM (FROM A MEDAL OF AGRIPPINA).

The Marcian fury (Virginia, 207).—The name is commonly given as *Caius* Marcius; but there were really no such names as *Caius* and *Cnæus*, the proper spelling being *Gaius* and *Gnæus*. The abbreviations, however, are *C.* and *Cn.*, going back to the time when *C* stood for both *C* and *G*.

Their cars (Virginia, 263).—A two-wheeled covered carriage (*carpentum*) was used to convey the Roman matrons in festal processions. The privilege of riding in a car on such occasions was a high distinction conferred on certain ladies by special grant of the senate. The vehicle was commonly drawn by a pair of mules, but sometimes by oxen or horses.

The serpent for a hand (Capys, 204).—The passages from Lucretius referred to by Macaulay (p. 182, footnote), read as follows (ii. 536):

> "Sicut quadripedum cum primis esse videmus
> In genere anguimanus elephantos, India quorum
> Milibus e multis vallo munitur eburno,
> Ut penitus nequeat penetrari : tanta ferarum
> Vis est, quarum nos perpauca exampla videmus."

and (v. 1302):

> "Inde boves lucas turrito corpore, taetras,
> Anguimanus, belli docuerunt volnera Poeni
> Sufferre et magnas Martis turbare catervas."

Manius Curius (Capys, 249).—Cf. Cicero, *De Senectute*, 16. 55 : "Ergo in hac [rustica] vita M.' Curius, cum de Samnitibus, de Sabinis, de Pyrrho triumphavisset, consumpsit extremum tempus aetatis; cuius quidem ego villam contemplans, abest enim non longe a me, admirari satis non possum vel hominis ipsius continentiam vel temporum disciplinam. Curio ad focum sedenti magnum auri pondus Samnites cum attulissent repudiati sunt ; non enim aurum habere praeclarum sibi videri dixit, sed eis qui haberent aurum imperare."

JUPITER.

INDEX OF WORDS AND PHRASES EXPLAINED.

SIDON.

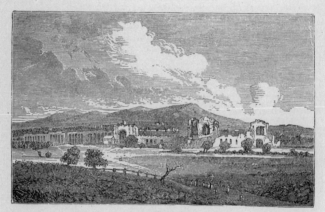

ALBAN HILLS.

ROLFE'S ENGLISH CLASSICS

Edited by WILLIAM J. ROLFE, Litt. D.

Each, $0.56

BROWNING'S SELECT POEMS

Twenty poems (including " Pippa Passes "), with Introduction, Life of Browning, Chronological Table of His Works, List of Books useful in studying them, Critical Comments, and Notes.

BROWNING'S SELECT DRAMAS

" A Blot in the 'Scutcheon," " Colombe's Birthday," and " A Soul's Tragedy "—with Introduction, Critical Comments, and Notes.

GOLDSMITH'S SELECT POEMS

" The Traveller," " The Deserted Village," and " Retaliation," with Life of Goldsmith, Recollections and Criticisms by Thackeray, Coleman the Younger, Campbell, Forster, and Irving, and Notes.

GRAY'S SELECT POEMS

The " Elegy," " The Bard," " The Progress of Poesy," and other Poems, with Life of Gray, William Howitt's Description of Stoke-Pogis, and historical, critical, and explanatory Notes.

MACAULAY'S LAYS OF ANCIENT ROME

With the Author's Preface and Introductions, Criticisms by John Stuart Mill, Henry Morley, " Christopher North," and others, historical and explanatory Notes, and copious Illustrations.

MILTON'S MINOR POEMS

All of Milton's Minor Poems except the Translations, with biographical and critical Introductions, and historical and explanatory Notes.

WORDSWORTH'S SELECT POEMS

Seventy-one Poems, with Life, Criticisms from Matthew Arnold, R. H. Hutton, Principal Shairp, J. R. Lowell, and Papers of the Wordsworth Society, and very full Notes. Illustrated by Abbey, Parsons, and other eminent artists.

AMERICAN BOOK COMPANY

(S. 96)

NEW ROLFE SHAKESPEARE

Edited by WILLIAM J. ROLFE, Litt.D.

40 volumes, each, $0.56

THE popularity of Rolfe's Shakespeare has been extraordinary. Since its first publication in 1870-83 it has been used more widely, both in schools and colleges, and by the general reading public, than any similar edition ever issued. It is to-day the standard annotated edition of Shakespeare for educational purposes.

¶ As teacher and lecturer Dr. Rolfe has been constantly in touch with the recent notable advances made in Shakespearian investigation and criticism ; and this revised edition he has carefully adjusted to present conditions.

¶ The introductions and appendices have been entirely rewritten, and now contain the history of the plays and poems; an account of the sources of the plots, with copious extracts from the chronicles and novels from which the poet drew his material ; and general comments by the editor, with selections from the best English and foreign criticism.

¶ The notes are very full, and include all the historical, critical, and illustrative material needed by the teacher, as well as by the student, and general reader. Special features in the notes are the extent to which Shakespeare is made to explain himself by parallel passages from his works; the frequent Bible illustrations; the full explanations of allusions to the manners and customs of the period; and descriptions of the localities connected with the poet's life and works.

¶ New notes have also been substituted for those referring to other volumes of the edition, so that each volume is now absolutely complete in itself. The form of the books has been modified, the page being made smaller to adjust them to pocket use.

AMERICAN BOOK COMPANY

(S. 97)

A HISTORY OF ENGLISH LITERATURE

By REUBEN POST HALLECK, M.A. (Yale),
Louisville Male High School. Price, $1.25

HALLECK'S HISTORY OF ENGLISH LITERATURE traces the development of that literature from the earliest times to the present in a concise, interesting, and stimulating manner. Although the subject is presented so clearly that it can be readily comprehended by high school pupils, the treatment is sufficiently philosophic and suggestive for any student beginning the study.

¶ The book is a history of literature, and not a mere collection of biographical sketches. Only enough of the facts of an author's life are given to make students interested in him as a personality, and to show how his environment affected his work. Each author's productions, their relations to the age, and the reasons why they hold a position in literature, receive adequate treatment.

¶ One of the most striking features of the work consists in the way in which literary movements are clearly outlined at the beginning of each chapter. Special attention is given to the essential qualities which differentiate one period from another, and to the animating spirit of each age. The author shows that each period has contributed something definite to the literature of England.

¶ At the end of each chapter a carefully prepared list of books is given to direct the student in studying the original works of the authors treated. He is told not only what to read, but also where to find it at the least cost. The book contains a special literary map of England in colors.

AMERICAN BOOK COMPANY

(S. 90)

INTRODUCTION TO AMERICAN LITERATURE

By BRANDER MATTHEWS, A.M., LL.B., Professor of Literature, Columbia University.   Price, $1.00

EX-PRESIDENT ROOSEVELT, in a most appreciative review in *The Bookman*, says: "The book is a piece of work as good of its kind as any American scholar has ever had in his hands. It is just the kind of book that should be given to a beginner, because it will give him a clear idea of what to read, and of the relative importance of the authors he is to read; yet it is much more than merely a book for beginners. Any student of the subject who wishes to do good work hereafter must not only read Mr. Matthews' book, but must largely adopt Mr. Matthews' way of looking at things, for these simply written, unpretentious chapters are worth many times as much as the ponderous tomes which contain what usually passes for criticism; and the principles upon which Mr. Matthews insists with such quiet force and good taste are those which must be adopted, not only by every student of American writings, but by ever American writer, if he is going to do what is really worth doing. . . . In short, Mr. Matthews has produced an admirable book, both in manner and matter, and has made a distinct addition to the very literature of which he writes."

¶ The book is amply provided with pedagogical features. Each chapter includes questions for review, bibliographical notes, facsimiles of manuscripts, and portraits, while at the end of the volume is a brief chronology of American literature.

AMERICAN BOOK COMPANY

(S. 91)

COMPOSITION-RHETORIC

By STRATTON D. BROOKS, Superintendent of
Schools, Boston, Mass., and MARIETTA HUB-
BARD, formerly English Department, High School,
La Salle, Ill.   Price, $1.00

THE fundamental aim of this volume is to enable pupils
to express their thoughts freely, clearly, and forcibly.
At the same time it is designed to cultivate literary
appreciation, and to develop some knowledge of rhetorical
theory.   The work follows closely the requirements of the
College Entrance Examination Board, and of the New
York State Education Department.

¶ In Part One are given the elements of description, narra-
tion, exposition, and argument; also special chapters on let-
ter-writing and poetry. A more complete and comprehensive
treatment of the four forms of discourse already discussed is
furnished in Part Two.   In each part is presented a series of
themes covering these subjects, the purpose being to give the
pupil inspiration, and that confidence in himself which comes
from the frequent repetition of an act.   A single new principle is introduced into each theme, and this is developed in
the text, and illustrated by carefully selected examples.

¶ The pupils are taught how to correct their own errors,
and also how to get the main thought in preparing their
lessons.   Careful coördination with the study of literature
and with other school studies is made throughout the book.

¶ The modern character of the illustrative extracts can not
fail to interest every boy and girl.   Concise summaries are
given following the treatment of the various forms of discourse,
and toward the end of the book there is a very comprehensive
and compact summary of grammatical principles. More than
usual attention is devoted to the treatment of argument.

AMERICAN BOOK COMPANY
(S. 88)

INTRODUCTORY COURSE IN ARGUMENTATION

By FRANCES M. PERRY, Instructor in English in Wellesley College. Price, $1.00

AN INTRODUCTORY COURSE IN ARGUMENTATION is intended for those who have not previously studied the subject, but while it makes a firm foundation for students who may wish to continue it, the volume is complete in itself. It is adapted for use in the first years of college or in the upper classes of secondary schools.

¶ The subject has been simplified as much as has been possible without lessening its educative value, yet no difficulties have been slighted. The beginner is set to work to exercise his reasoning power on familiar material and without the added difficulty of research. Persuasion has not been considered until conviction is fully understood. The two methods in use in teaching argumentation—the brief-drawing method and the syllogistic method—have been combined, so that the one will help the student to grasp the other.

¶ The volume is planned and proportioned with the expectation that it will be closely followed as a text-book rather than used to supplement an independent method of presentation. To that end each successive step is given explicit exposition and full illustration, and carefully graded exercises are provided to test the student's understanding of an idea, and fix it in his memory.

¶ The course is presented in three divisions; the first relating to finding and formulating the proposition for argument, the second to proving the proposition, and the last, to finding the material to prove the proposition—research.

AMERICAN BOOK COMPANY
(S. 103)

ESSENTIALS IN HISTORY

ESSENTIALS IN ANCIENT HISTORY . $1.50
> From the earliest records to Charlemagne. By
> ARTHUR MAYER WOLFSON, Ph.D., First
> Assistant in History, DeWitt Clinton High School,
> New York

ESSENTIALS IN MEDIÆVAL AND MODERN
HISTORY $1.50
> From Charlemagne to the present day. By SAMUEL
> BANNISTER HARDING, Ph.D., Professor of
> European History, Indiana University

ESSENTIALS IN ENGLISH HISTORY . $1.50
> From the earliest records to the present day. By
> ALBERT PERRY WALKER, A.M., Master in
> History, English High School, Boston

ESSENTIALS IN AMERICAN HISTORY . $1.50
> From the discovery to the present day. By ALBERT
> BUSHNELL HART, LL.D., Professor of History,
> Harvard University

THESE volumes correspond to the four subdivisions
required by the College Entrance Examination
Board, and by the New York State Education Department. Each volume is designed for one year's work.
Each of the writers is a trained historical scholar, familiar
with the conditions and needs of secondary schools.

¶ The effort has been to deal only with the things which
are typical and characteristic; to avoid names and details
which have small significance, in order to deal more justly
with the forces which have really directed and governed
mankind. Especial attention is paid to social history.

¶ The books are readable and teachable, and furnish brief
but useful sets of bibliographies and suggestive questions.
No pains have been spared by maps and pictures to furnish
a significant and thorough body of illustration.

AMERICAN BOOK COMPANY
(S. 130)

HISTORY OF ENGLISH AND AMERICAN LITERATURE

By CHARLES F. JOHNSON, L.H.D., Professor of English Literature, Trinity College, Hartford.   Price, $1.25

A TEXT-BOOK for a year's course in schools and colleges, in which English literary history is regarded as composed of periods, each marked by a definite tone of thought and manner of expression. The treatment follows the divisions logically and systematically, without any of the perplexing cross divisions so frequently made. It is based on the historic method of study, and refers briefly to events in each period bearing on social development, to changes in religious and political theory, and even to advances in the industrial arts.   In addition, the book contains critiques, general surveys, summaries, biographical sketches, bibliographies, and suggestive questions.   The examples have been chosen from poems which are generally familiar, and of an illustrative character.

JOHNSON'S FORMS OF ENGLISH POETRY
$1.00

T HIS book contains nothing more than every young person should know about the construction of English verse, and its main divisions, both by forms and by subject-matter.   The historical development of the main divisions is sketched, and briefly illustrated by representative examples ; but the true character of poetry as an art and as a social force has always been in the writer's mind.   Only the elements of prosody are given.   The aim has been not to make the study too technical, but to interest the student in poetry, and to aid him in acquiring a well-rooted taste for good literature.

AMERICAN BOOK COMPANY
(S. 101)

Fight between
Mamilius, and Herm-
~~inius, with the flight~~
~~of Mamilius horse.~~

fight between Mamilus an ~~Aut~~
Aulus takes B. A., the Twin B.
The twin B. take news to

Tribunes . of Roman

One Page.